Thomas Aquinas on Risk in Economic Activity

Pierre Januard

Thomas Aquinas on Risk in Economic Activity

Mapping, Typologies, and Dynamic Structure

palgrave
macmillan

Pierre Januard
Maison des Sciences économiques
Université Paris 1 Panthéon-Sorbonne
Paris, France

ISBN 978-3-031-83824-8 ISBN 978-3-031-83825-5 (eBook)
https://doi.org/10.1007/978-3-031-83825-5

This Palgrave Macmillan imprint is published by the registered company Springer Nature Switzerland AG.
The registered company address is: Gewerbestrasse 11, 6330 Cham, Switzerland

To my father, Jean-Pierre Januard (1940–1993)

Foreword

"Thomas Aquinas on risk in economic activity": what can a Dominican from eight centuries ago, and evidently not an economist, have to say to us about "risks" when the very word does not appear in his writings? Pierre Januard, himself certainly an economist, takes up the challenge—and succeeds—in building a bridge to the twenty-first century and our present challenges. Today, risk and uncertainty are everywhere, and on the increase: geopolitical risk, climate risk, cyber risk, financial risk ... Such are the primary concerns not only of economists but also—as I can testify—of public leaders and entrepreneurs alike.

We have mathematised risk, yet we also need to think about it, to take a step back. Quantification sometimes seems to obviate the need for in-depth reflection on the nature of this risk, so omnipresent, and with which we are so familiar, yet of which we have so little understanding.

The history of economic thought, from a long-term perspective, helps us take this step back, since it permits us to see how, before the advent of probability calculations, reflection on risk became highly sophisticated. Such are the reflections of Thomas Aquinas, at the heart of the Middle Ages. It is this author who took the broadest possible approach to economic activities in all their diversity, and who, in so doing, displayed the multiplicity of risks.

Pierre Januard combines his mastery of economic analysis with his solid command of mediaeval thought to take us on a journey that is at the same time both erudite and educational. As well as his academic career as a teacher and researcher, his approach to risk is infused with experience, deriving from his professional responsibilities in capital markets as well as in the non-profit sector. This journey to the land of risk is at once both exotic and familiar. The cultural, political and economic context has changed, but the fundamental transactions remain the same, whether of buying and selling, or borrowing and lending. The thrust of the book is to show that risk is present for all agents and in all transactions. The lists of risks at the end of each chapter illustrate this in a very practical manner.

The investigation is extremely precise and meticulous. It is not just a description of risks but a rigorous economic analysis. The mapping of risks, their classifications and their lexicon highlights the fact that this vast panorama, rooted in a certain time and place—France and Italy of the thirteenth century—is possessed of something universal that we would do well to rediscover. Here, we find signs of objective tools for the analysis of risk: Aquinas takes an objective look, focusing not on the agent's intention, which is unknown to us, but on visible and public elements, such as the price.

Drawing upon the writings of Thomas Aquinas, Pierre Januard brings to light two fundamental risks that no doubt receive insufficient attention from us today. He shows that right from his first economic text, Thomas Aquinas addresses the risk of analysis, the risk of error on the part of the observer—yesterday the moralist, today the economist or manager. This is not so much the risk of calculation, with which we are familiar, but the more decisive risk of misunderstanding the very nature of the operation. Aquinas is calling into question the way in which his predecessors understood lending, and therefore the way in which, in his day, the prohibition of lending at interest was justified. While the example must be seen in the context of the Middle Ages, this approach is still very relevant today. To give just one example, crypto assets can be an investment object, albeit a risky one, but confusion arises if they claim to be a currency, regarding which they lack both the attribute of stability and the status as legal tender.

This risk echoes another fundamental risk of error, which concerns the very purpose of exchanging a given object. Many of today's pricing disputes appear to be quantitative, when in fact they involve an unspoken disagreement about what is being exchanged. The issue is particularly difficult when it comes to "public" goods: should a visit to the doctor, admission to a museum or even the supply of electricity be priced at cost, or according to their estimated social utility? And to assess this utility, should we differentiate according to people, their income levels or their different possible uses of the good?

To take the time to ask oneself about what one is exchanging and the nature of the economic transaction one is considering, and to bear in mind that one could be mistaken, are by no means unprofitable detours. This is, undoubtedly, itself an instrument for the reduction of risk. The typologies of all the economic risks with which we are familiar then take on their full meaning within a dynamic structure of risk, which Pierre Januard brings to light at the end of his analysis. I wish you an enjoyable read, in his company and in that of Thomas Aquinas.

Governor of the Banque de France
Paris, France

François Villeroy de Galhau

Acknowledgements

I would like to express my profound gratitude to all the individuals and institutions that supported the research presented in this book. First of all, to the directors of the Philosophy, History, and Analysis of Economic Representations (PHARE) research team at the University of Paris 1 Panthéon-Sorbonne, Prof. Laurent Jaffro, Prof. Goulven Rubin and Prof. Nathalie Sigot, who provided me with the material and academic resources necessary to carry out this research and for its publication; as well as Dr. Nadeera Rajapakse for her advice and expertise on the thought of Thomas Aquinas, Dr. Jean Dellemotte for his highly inspiring writings, Dr. Laurie Bréban for her insightful guidance, and all the members of the research team.

I would also like to extend my warmest thanks to the Rector Magnificus Thomas Joseph White, Dean Helen Alford and the Faculty of Social Sciences of the Pontifical University of St. Thomas Aquinas (*Angelicum*) for their confidence in me.

I am grateful to President Adriano Oliva, Dr. Timothy Bellamah and all the members of the *Commissio Leonina* for the care with which they shared their invaluable knowledge of the works of Thomas Aquinas. I extend my thanks to Prof. Gilles Berceville, Dr. Jacques-Benoît Rauscher and Dr. Benedict Young for their wise counsel, enriched by their profound expertise in social sciences, philology and languages.

I also thank the anonymous referees, whose suggestions and comments helped me improve the manuscript, and my editor, Wyndham Hacket Pain, for his attentive support and guidance.

I would like to express special thanks to the Governor of the Banque de France, François Villeroy de Galhau, and to Professor Emeritus André Lapidus for kindly agreeing to write the foreword and afterword of this book. It is a great honour to benefit from their erudition, experience and friendship, which are truly invaluable.

Finally, I am deeply grateful to the PHARE research team, as well as the Cèdre Finance Éthique and the Centre d'Études du Saulchoir, for funding this research.

I have benefitted from numerous insights during the many discussions that followed the presentations of various parts of this work. However, any errors or oversights that may remain are my own, and I bear full responsibility for them.

Ethical Approval This study was performed in accordance with the principles of the Declaration of Helsinki.

Competing Interests The author has no competing interests to declare that are relevant to the content of this manuscript.

Contents

About the Author

Pierre Januard holds a doctorate in economics from the University of Paris 1 Panthéon-Sorbonne. He is an Associate Researcher in the PHARE research team at the University of Paris 1 Panthéon-Sorbonne and a Professor Aggregato at the Faculty of Social Sciences of the Pontifical University of St. Thomas Aquinas (*Angelicum*) in Rome. He has taught both economics and mediaeval thought in various institutions, including the Catholic University of the West in Angers, University Paris 1 Panthéon-Sorbonne and Le Mans University, and has been head of research in finance companies. He is managing director of the Centre d'Études du Saulchoir in Paris.

Abbreviations

Title Abbreviations

Quodl.	*Quodlibetal Questions*
Sent.	*Sentences* of Peter Lombard
S. T.	*Summa theologiae*

Subdivisions in Scholastic Works

a.	article
c.	chapter
d.	distinction
l.	book
obj.	objection
q.	question
qc.	sub-question
resp.	response
t.	title

List of Tables

CHAPTER 1

Introduction

Abstract The emblematic figure of economic thought in the Middle Ages, Thomas Aquinas (c. 1225–1274) is both its most prolific and its best-known contributor. He deals with economic activities in all their diversity and provides, sometimes explicitly and often implicitly, an in-depth analysis of economic risk. Even in the Middle Ages, risk was present in all operations and among all agents. Two main aspects of the elements of understanding of risk provided by Aquinas deserve our attention. Firstly, he highlights a risk that modern formal approaches based on probability distributions have relegated to the background, but which is in fact the risk that determines all the others: the risk of misunderstanding the nature of the activity being handled and the object being exchanged. Secondly, he deploys a multitude of situations involving risks. The diversity of the vocabulary used and the combinations that the classification of these risks makes possible provide analytical tools whose relevance goes beyond the historical framework of the Middle Ages and still speaks to us today.

Keywords Thomas Aquinas • Risk • Probability • Prudence • Danger

The emblematic figure of economic thought in the Middle Ages, Thomas Aquinas (c. 1225–1274), is both its most prolific and its best-known contributor. The thirteenth century marks a conceptual leap in economic

P. Januard, *Thomas Aquinas on Risk in Economic Activity*,
https://doi.org/10.1007/978-3-031-83825-5_1

understanding, and it is at the heart of this transformation that his writings must be positioned, coming after Robert of Courçon's *De usura* and William of Auxerre's *Summa aurea* at the beginning of that period, after the writings of his master Albert the Great in the middle decades, and before the *De usuris in communi* of his disciple Giles of Lessines, which came at the century's close.

Aquinas deals with economic activities in all their diversity and provides, sometimes explicitly and often implicitly, an in-depth analysis of economic risk. Such risk seems today to be omnipresent, whether we fear it or use it for gain, and it would be all too easy to believe that the emergence of risk is a fruit of the modern capitalist economy, and its present-day over-extension is a feature peculiar to the contemporary economy. On the contrary, however, an analysis of the works of Aquinas shows that even in the Middle Ages, risk was present in all operations and among all agents. Today we are comfortable referring to agents as "economic transactors" (Januard 1973, 18–19), which is consistent with Aquinas's exchange-focused approach to economic activity. In the eight hundred years that have elapsed since he was writing, the cultural, social and economic context has changed, but the fundamental transactions remain the same: buying and selling, lending and borrowing. These operations by their very nature are intrinsically risky. Although some aspects have changed, therefore, Aquinas's structural analysis transcends historical contingencies and remains relevant today.

This book, which addresses risk in economic matters in the works of Aquinas, aims to contribute to a history of economic thought within an economic analysis framework. Its aim will be achieved if it also provides historians, philosophers and theologians with support in mobilising the instruments of economic science for their own work on Aquinas, and if it supplies economists and practitioners involved in risk management, as well as philosophers or jurists who seek to understand and regulate risk, with instruments for its analysis and contextualisation.

Why Look at Aquinas's Thinking on Risk in Economic Activity?

The economic thought of Thomas Aquinas remains little known and is often underestimated by economists as well as by mediaevalists; to the former group, reflecting on the changes in socio-economic reality and the development of economic analysis over the last eight centuries, it seems too remote to bear any relevance; and to the latter, it appears of very minor interest compared with the philosophical and theological contributions of that celebrated author. Before going into the details of my research and its results, and soliciting further attention from the reader, I must therefore highlight the interest as well as the limitations of the Thomasian contribution to economic risk, concerning not only knowledge of mediaeval thought but also economic analysis and practice today. To this end, I will outline the main points to be elaborated in the course of the book.

Two main aspects of the elements of understanding risk provided by Aquinas deserve our attention. Firstly, he highlights a risk that modern formal approaches based on probability distributions have relegated to the background, but which is in fact the risk that determines all others: the risk of misunderstanding the nature of the activity being handled and the object being exchanged. Secondly, he deploys a multitude of situations involving risks. The diversity of the vocabulary used and the combinations that the classification of these risks makes possible provide analytical tools whose relevance goes beyond the historical framework of the Middle Ages and still speaks to us today.

Rediscovering Risks on Understanding Activities and Goods

Today, a technical distinction is made between *risk*, which can be calculated via given probabilities, and *uncertainty*, where probabilities are not given. Since the calculation of probability only really appeared in modern times, one might prefer the notion of uncertainty to account for the situations described by Thomas Aquinas. However, the term "risk", taken in its current sense, seems more relevant, because it is situated upstream of the question of the possibility of its calculation. Moreover, while risk, in its technical sense, may involve a risk of both winning or losing, in everyday language, it retains the negative connotation of risk of loss, which is consistent with Aquinas's approach.

Aquinas highlights two fundamental risks that are often neglected or minimised by contemporary economics. The first is a risk connected to the analysis itself, that is, the risk of misunderstanding the transaction we are dealing with. In his very first economic text, the passage on usury in his great early work the *Commentary on the Sentences*, Aquinas introduces the idea that his predecessors' understanding of usury is probably true but not certainly so. Economists are familiar with considering errors in the collection of data or the development of quantitative models but not always with considering errors as significant as those which concern Aquinas. He considers it probable but not certain that the loan should be considered as a Roman *mutuum*. This model involves a transfer of ownership, with the borrower now owning the sum and therefore also assuming the risk, since it is on him that the risk rests, and no longer on the lender. To consider that this statement could be false is to consider that we could be mistaken about the identity of the owner and the person who incurs the risk. It also means considering whether one of the key attractions of this understanding of money loan, namely that it involves no interest, might also be an error and is thereby depriving the economy of a desirable means of financing.

This also implies considering that a group of agents, in this case usurers, might not have to find themselves in the situation of opprobrium in which they are placed. Today, the determination of the very nature of the activity is sometimes neglected in favour of its quantitative treatment. However, without first determining the licitness of the activity, and hence the appropriate legal framework, the corresponding tax regime and the various risks associated with this activity which weigh upon the agents involved, any considerations regarding the conduct of the operation are likely to be irrelevant.

After the risk of analysis relating to the nature of the activity, Aquinas highlights a risk of analysis relating to the nature of the object exchanged. The same text—his first economic text, the passage on usury of the *Commentary on the Sentences*—that considers probable but not certain the hypothesis according to which the loan is a Roman *mutuum*, also presents a conception of money that he considers erroneous. This initial inquiry, prior to any practical application, into the nature of money proves particularly relevant today, notably in light of the rise of cryptocurrencies. For one may be tempted to focus too quickly on the quantitative aspects of their emergence, such as their volatility or the amounts they represent, when what is fundamentally at stake is an understanding of their nature—whether they constitute currencies, in the monetary sense, or financial assets. This attention to the nature of the thing might appear more philosophical than economic, and seemingly distant from the concerns of those involved with cryptocurrencies; however, it has very tangible implications, bearing on the determination of their legal framework, the supervisory and regulatory authorities charged with overseeing them, and the management techniques to be applied.

Aquinas later theorised more generally that it is the nature of the thing, its *quid*, that determines the nature of the exchange and of the exchange ratio (price, stipend …) that corresponds to it. Aquinas is very imaginative in proposing a multitude of exchange ratios, each corresponding to the nature of the good or service. While price, which corresponds to an exchange of equal values, is the most common, there is also the family of stipends, understood as non-proportional compensation that allows the activity to continue. This family is vast, with a multitude of specific names depending on whether it concerns the soldier, the priest, the actor, the lender or even the merchant. There are also cases where the specific nature of the service requires a multi-factor calculation formula: lawyers and medical doctors, for example, are paid according to the work involved, the difficulty of the case, the client's financial capacity and local customs.

Without a proper determination of the nature of the object, the terms of the exchange could once again become irrelevant, hence leading to conflict. Most pricing disputes today concerning specific goods and services—such as medical services, basic necessities or energy—give rise to quantitative debates about price levels. However, very often the issue lies upstream, in establishing a consensus on the nature of the good or service and the nature of the exchange ratio associated with it.

Analysis Instruments: Naming and Classifying Risks

Thomasian analysis is useful today not only for its attention to goods and activities but also for its ability to name and classify risks and to approach the broad notion of risk via different paths. The absence of the word "risk" obliges Thomas Aquinas to develop a set of concepts and lexicons related to risk, each of which develops a facet of it. We thus see the emergence of the notion of probability, not in the sense of the calculation of probability, as would be the case a few centuries later, but of the distinction between what is certain and what is probable, and between what is believed to be true and what is not: the probable is what we believe to be true but are not certain of. Today's highly sophisticated calculation of risk might seem to relegate such old approaches to the history of ideas, and certainly, if we look in Aquinas's writings for quantitative elements, we are likely to be disappointed. However, maintaining the radical distinction between what is probable, although it has so far occurred systematically, or a thesis that can be persuasively argued—and what is certain—that is to say, demonstrable apodictically and hence free of any form of risk—would be very useful. It would certainly save a lot of trouble for all those who have been certain that economic catastrophe would not happen, because it was infinitesimally probable.

Yet, the quantitative dimension of probability is not entirely absent. In describing economic activity, Aquinas often uses the notion of estimation in the sense of an approximation. This is the case with determining a just price, which can only be done with a margin of error. Human beings do not have the capacity to find exactly and immediately the right price that satisfies the parties and ensures that the exchange will go through. Admittedly, Aquinas considers that most of the time, the difference is small and does not cast doubt upon the justice of the exchange, but the risk is nevertheless inherent in any exchange. Here again, remembering this oft-forgotten precept would guide not only economists but every economic agent, and even in the most quotidian operations, towards a better awareness of their own ignorance and their own inability to exchange without risk.

Aquinas then discusses prudence in business, or rather imprudence, which can occur either through negligence, that is, lack of attention, or through incompetence, that is, lack of anticipation or failure to take account of one's inability to anticipate. This behaviour, which increases the risk of loss, leads to overspending and poor cost management. Although modern science of management enables much more sophisticated analyses than Aquinas's, we are perhaps paying less attention to the cause of the problem. Aquinas is no great help in measuring the extent of management errors quantitatively, but by distinguishing between these two forms of imprudence, he helps us identify their origin. And that is the first step towards remedying the problem.

Finally, Aquinas sees risk primarily in its negative aspect, as a danger. Today, risk is understood as a possibility of loss or gain and can arouse a certain attraction. It is indeed itself an object of exchange and has an economic substance of its own. Yet Aquinas reminds us that risk is not a good or an activity in itself, but something that characterises them. It always has a basis or support, which is the object of exchange. An activity can be very risky, like that of merchants who are threatened with shipwreck or robbery, and this can justify an increase in the selling price and therefore a profit. Yet, for Aquinas, the purpose of the merchant's activity is not to sell risk but rather to supply the country while also earning a living to feed his own family and to help the poor. The use of the word "danger" here is a reminder of the origins of the notion of risk, which always involves a dangerous element.

The many risky situations described by Aquinas bring into play a wide variety of risks, which can be classified in a number of ways. These categories can then be cross-referenced to arrive at typologies, the level of elaboration of which enables a detailed analysis of the notion of risk. Risk can be classified according to activity, such as loan, commercial exchange or limit cases of market exchange; according to whether it is a quantitative or qualitative risk; according to whether it is an error in understanding the transaction, a commercial risk imposed by external conditions on the co-contractors, or a strategic risk, which is an internal risk arising from the lack of information on the co-contractor's intention. Risks can also be distinguished according to whether the risk relates to the licitness of the activity, the conditions under which it is carried out or a remuneration risk. Finally, a distinction must be made between risks explicitly named by Aquinas, risks implicitly deducible from the situation described and the risks induced by Aquinas's treatment of the situation.

The concrete manifestations of risk may have changed over the last eight hundred years, but the analytical grid remains profoundly relevant today, as it enables us to characterise all the risks associated with trade. All those involved in risk analysis can benefit from taking a step back from calculating the probabilities of gain or loss to attain a deeper understanding of these risks, their proximities and their interactions. More broadly, the aim of this book is to take a new look at activities that, although thought to be recent, are in fact often simply variations on practices that are very old.

Aquinas's Economic Thought: A Vast Theoretical Investigation Informed by a Travelling Life

Thomas Aquinas spent his life on the road. Although he did not come from a merchant family, like the merchants, he travelled the roads of Europe. We know little about his practical experience of economic life, but the situations he describes are consistent with what historians report. His theoretical thinking, which is highly developed both in terms of the diversity of the subjects tackled and its speculative nature, is therefore rooted in a solid knowledge of the socio-economic reality of his time. His thinking evolves from his early writings to his major work, the *Summa theologiae*. Starting with the lesser-known writings of his youth thus provides new insights into Aquinas's economic thought.

Thomas Aquinas: A Brief History

To understand Aquinas's view of economic activity, we must look at his own history. Thomas Aquinas's family can be traced back as far as 887 and is known to have owned the castle of Roccasecca, in the county of Aquino about halfway between Rome and Naples, since the end of the tenth century. Aquinas's father was a knight, as were his brothers. One of his brothers had taken part in an expedition to the Holy Land and served in the army of Frederic II, but was later executed for plotting his death and supporting the Pope. His father is identifiable on the obituary of the abbey of Monte Cassino as a *miles*, cavalry soldier, or, in a mediaeval context, a knight (Weisheipl [1974] 1993, 16–19; Torrell 2015, 20–25). Aquinas's familiarity with the lexicon of chivalry may indicate a *chevalier manqué* (Synan 1988, 437); and it is not surprising that he conceived of the social order as aristocratic, in which the disgraced knight falls to the ranks of peasants and merchants (*S. T.*, Ia IIae, q. 91, a. 6, resp.; Synan 1988, 419–420), and in which merchants lead a life of pleasure that encourages psychological and moral weakness (*De regno*, II, 7 (II, 3)).

While some details of Aquinas's life and some dates remain under discussion, biographers agree on the main elements of his story (see e.g. Weisheipl [1974] 1993; Tugwell 1988; Torrell 2012; Torrell 2015; Imbach and Oliva 2009; Porro 2015; not forgetting, for its character as a hagiographic source, the account of his first biographer, William of Tocco, the *Ystoria sancti Thome de Aquino*, written between 1318 and 1323). Aquinas was born around 1225, became an oblate at the nearby monastery of Monte Cassino at the age of five or six, then left for Naples in the autumn of 1239 to continue his studies, entering the Dominican order there in 1244. He was kidnapped by his brothers at his mother's request and taken back to Roccasecca where the family, who hoped to make him the future abbot of Monte Cassino, tried to change his mind. In the summer of 1245, he returned to the Dominican convent in Naples (escaping, according to some sources; or more probably being finally set free by his family). In spite of these events, Aquinas remained closely linked to his family. He was then sent to Paris for a first three-year period of study, probably attending the classes of Albert the Great, with whom in 1248 he left for Cologne, remaining there until 1252. This stay is better attested in the sources. He continued his theological studies with Albert, and in 1252, on Albert's advice and with the support of the Dominican cardinal Hugh of Saint-Cher, the Master of the Dominican Order sent Aquinas to

Paris, probably still as a bachelor of biblical studies and then as a bachelor of the *Sentences*, to teach the *Sentences* of Peter Lombard, according to the academic practice of the time, despite his young age. Aquinas received his *licentia docendi* and presented his inaugural lecture in 1256, earlier than the age of 35 required by the university statutes, and despite the fact that his own *Commentary on the Sentences* had not yet been completed.

Aquinas probably left for Italy in 1259, likely for Naples, but the period 1259–1261 remains uncertain. He was assigned to Orvieto in 1261, where he was a lector in the convent, responsible for the ongoing formation of the Dominican friars, and then to Rome in 1265 to take over the initial formation of the young friars. It was for this purpose that he began a year later to write the *Summa theologiae*. He returned to Paris, probably in 1268, and resumed his teaching there. The reasons for this return are debated and presumably cumulative: the presence of conservative theologians who saw Aristotle as a danger to the faith; the influence attributed to the Averroists whose errors had to be refuted; and pressure from secularists who wanted to exclude mendicants (Dominicans and Franciscans) from university teaching. In 1272, he left for Naples. Around 6 December 1273, Aquinas is said to have had a spiritual experience while celebrating Mass. From that day onwards, he appeared profoundly changed and ceased to write, reportedly declaring: "I can no longer. All that I have written seems to me to be straw compared to what I have seen" (Torrell 2015, 370). Early in the new year, in response to a summons by Pope Gregory IX, he set off to the Council of Lyon which was to be held on 1 May 1274. What followed was tragic and has been taken up in his hagiography. Lost in thought while walking, he hit his head on a branch of a tree that had fallen on the road. At the end of February, resting at the home of his niece, for he was already ill, he is said to have asked for fresh herrings (William of Tocco, *Ystoria*, c. 56, 115–116), which gave rise to the legend that this was his favourite dish. He returned to the abbey of Fossanova, but his illness worsened, and he died there on 7 March 1274—"the only date in his life of which we can be certain" (Weisheipl [1974] 1993, 7).

Aquinas on Economic Activity

Alongside a life of study, prayer and teaching, Thomas Aquinas travelled extensively and had occasion to observe the socio-economic changes of his time, both in terms of urbanisation and of the circulation of professional merchants throughout Europe. The thirteenth century saw the development of the great European trade routes, the maritime routes from the great ports as well as land and river routes between Flanders and Venice and then along the Seine valley (Ellul 2013, 201). Large regular fairs, particularly in Champagne, set the pace for the economic life of Europe and the life of merchants: Lagny in January–February, Bar-sur-Aube in March–April, Provins in May–June, Troyes in July–August, Provins in September–November and Troyes in September–November (Le Goff [2010] 2019, 30). Fairs were true institutions, endowed with their own legal personality and privileges. It was a time of urbanisation, with the rising cities bringing new energy to crafts, trades and local markets (Ellul 2013, 224–225), and stimulating the emergence of a new class, that of professional merchants, well versed in accounting, currency exchange, navigation and commercial law. While Aquinas does not give a direct account of what he observed of economic activity, his theoretical writings are informed not only by the pastoral questions he was asked and the testimonies he received, but also by what his personal history, his movements and his travels had given him the opportunity to see.

Thus, although economic activity does not lie at the heart of Aquinas's thought, it nevertheless becomes an important part of his cultural universe, through the theoretical contributions of his predecessors (his first treatise on usury sets out a *status quaestionis*), by the questions put to him (his treatises on forward sales and on the use by the prince of the taxes levied on usury earnings were written in response to questions), and by his observations of the world of his time (several times he travelled the same routes as the merchants he describes, who came from Italy to sell cloth at the Lagny fair near Paris).

Quantitatively speaking, Aquinas's texts with an economic scope constitute a minor part of his work. But although the motivation for these texts is primarily moral, since they deal with the sinfulness of the agent who takes part in a transaction, Aquinas's contribution to the understanding of economic mechanisms and transactions should not be underestimated. His input has often been summarised as engendering a new or deeper understanding of the just price and usury, yet it is in fact much broader in scope than this and leads ultimately to a unified understanding of economic activity, although each activity is treated in a specific way in separate texts.

Moreover, commentators often approach Aquinas's economic thought as a unified whole, referring mainly to his later works, and especially the two economic questions in the *Summa theologiae* (*S. T.*, IIa IIae, q. 77 and 78). However, Aquinas's economic contributions can be divided into two main stages. The first stage consists of his early works, the *Commentary on the Sentences* in 1254–1256 (*In III Sent.*, d. 37, a. 6 on usury and *In IV Sent.*, d. 16, q. 4, a. 2, qc. 3 on the activity of merchants) and *De emptione et venditione ad tempus*, a brief letter on forward sales (1262). To this can be added the passage on trade from *De regno* (II, 7 (II, 3)), which probably dates from 1265, although this work is primarily political, is chronologically intermediate and involves attribution difficulties, at least for the parts following this economic chapter. The second stage is made up of late or mature works, dating from the years 1269–1273: the *Letter to the Duchess of Brabant* (*Ad ducissam Brabantiae*), *De malo* (q. 13, a. 4), *Quodlibetal Questions* (*III Quodl.*, q. 7, a. 2), and the *Summa theologiae* (IIa IIae, q. 78) on usury; *Quodlibetal Questions* (*II Quodl.*, q. 5, a. 2) and the *Summa theologiae* (IIa IIae, q. 77), as well as a passage from the commentary on Aristotle's *Nicomachean Ethics* (*Ethicorum*, V, 9) on the activity of the merchant, exchange and just price; and a passage on money from the commentary on Aristotle's *Politics* (*Politicorum*, I, 7–8).

Referring to the early works is of threefold interest: firstly, while they show his filiations, they also manifest Aquinas's freedom from the authorities and the novelty of his approach compared to that of his predecessors. Secondly, they provide new keys to understanding the more well-known works such as the *Summa theologiae*. Finally, they contain elements of their own that are not explicitly present in the later works, but which nevertheless constitute major contributions. It should also be emphasised that Aquinas's economic thought is not only to be found in the texts specifically dedicated to that topic but also in the more spiritual or theological texts, since it is there that the notion of just price, central to Aquinas's thought, would be developed. This notion was only implicitly integrated into the early works, before being taken up explicitly in the later economic texts. I must therefore add to the early works that are properly economic the three passages containing the first occurrences of the expression "just price" in the *Commentary on the Book of Isaiah* (*Super Isaiam*, 55, 1), Aquinas's first real theological work, probably written in Paris in 1252 as a biblical bachelor (Torrell 2015, 53–54, following Oliva 2006), and in the treatise on the sacraments of the *Commentary on the Sentences* (*In IV Sent.*, d. 25, q. 3, a. 1, qc. 1 and *In IV Sent.*, d. 36, q. 1, a. 2).

Aquinas's Approach to Risk in Economic Activity

Thomas Aquinas does not propose a unified theory of risk, but it is possible to reconstruct analytical instruments and results applied to concrete situations. The vocabulary he employs, and even more so the concepts it designates, as well as the classification of risks using cross-cutting typologies, provide a sophisticated analytical framework, allowing us above all to arrive at a representation of a dynamic structure of risk, a representation that gives a synoptic account of the profusion of Aquinas's thoughts on risk.

A Wide-Range Lexicon and Approach to Risk

One of the keys to understanding these early works is the notion of risk. Aquinas uses a wide lexicon to evoke risk in economic activity: probability and estimation, prudence and danger (Januard 2024).

Being concerned above all with moral issues, Aquinas seeks to determine the conditions for justice in exchange, whether as regards lending or commercial activity. As the agents' intentions remain hidden, the price is to serve, at first implicitly and later explicitly, as a visible and objective indicator of the justice of an exchange, and so to reduce the risk of injustice. Aquinas also expresses the risk on achievement of activity, such as transport, which may be subject to dangers.

Aquinas is situated upstream of the calculus of probabilities and the conception of probability as a "degree of certainty" developed by Jacob Bernoulli in 1713 in his *Ars conjectandi* (IV, 1, p. 211 and IV, 4, p. 225) precisely in order to address the need to measure risk within economic activity. However, each of the situations described by Aquinas involves a set of risks that affect either the observer or each of the parties involved. Risk, in its modern meaning, corresponds to a random variable, that is, a function going from states of the world to a set of consequences; and while the formalisation of such a function and the calculation of probabilities obviously remain absent in Aquinas's work, situations that would be described today in terms of a random variable do nevertheless exist and he does treat of them.

Before proceeding further, I need to explain why I prefer to use the term "risk", whereas the term "uncertainty" is often used to describe mediaeval economic risk (e.g. Ernst 2016, 128), as there is as yet no role for calculation, and the distinction that is made is between what is certain and what is not. Aquinas, however, is upstream of Knight's (1921, 233) distinctions between a "risk" that would be calculable and an "uncertainty" that would not, and of the new clarifications provided by Savage (1954). The lexicon of "uncertainty", in seeking to bypass the notion of calculating probability that the modern meaning of "risk" entails, introduces a modern specification absent from Aquinas's texts, where the question is not about the possibility of a calculation but about the existence of a plurality of possible consequences. It therefore seems preferable to retain the term "risk" in its most general sense.

The first economic text of Aquinas, on usury, introduces the risk of error in the analysis of the operation through the notion of *probability*, by the expression "rather/enough probable [*satis probabilis*]" (*In III Sent.*, d. 37, a. 6, resp.). Thus, in using this phrase, Aquinas seems to challenge his predecessors' understanding of monetary lending. This reading may be debatable, according to what we know of the meaning of *satis* and *probabilis* in Aquinas's time. In the Middle Ages, "*probabilis*" may characterise a class of propositions held to be true (Schuessler 2019, 22–59). However, probability is not a degree of certainty, as it would be for Jacob Bernoulli five centuries later, but rather, following Aristotle's *Posterior Analytics*, "probable" and "certain" are deemed to refer to two different orders of knowledge (Byrne 1968; Daston 1988; Hacking 2006). In addition, "*satis*" may bear a connotation of ambivalence, and some elements in this passage seem to confirm that the use of "*satis probabilis*" expresses a kind of doubt, or at least raises a possibility of error.

As well as the notion of probability, Aquinas introduced the notion of estimation, using "*aestimatio*" to refer to the approximations that agents make when they try to find the just price on the market (*De emptione*, I; and later in *S. T.*, IIa IIae, q. 77, a. 1, ad 1). This also involves a risk of error.

De emptione then also resorts to a second lexicon, that of *prudence*, to evoke the risk incurred by the merchant, who makes expenses without the sale being certain, and the risk of injustice in the price if via that price he passes on illicit expenses, that is, those made "without precaution [*incaute*] and unwisely [*imprudenter*]" (*De emptione*, III). In the Middle Ages, prudence is a virtue, not a statistical concept leading to calculation (Yuengert 2012, 57, 74–75; Hirschfeld 2018, 179). However, Aquinas's analysis is in line with contemporary approaches to prudence, where imprudence means increasing the risk of loss (Kimball 1990). Aquinas here introduces a twofold risk of bad management: negligence and incompetence, which translates into an inability to plan ahead.

Finally, later works will engage the lexicon of *danger*, through words such as *discrimen* and *periculum*, used to express the risk of transport and supply (*De regno*, II, 7 (II, 3); *S. T.*, IIa IIae, q. 77, a. 3, resp. and ad 3, and *S. T.*, IIa IIae, q. 77, a. 4, ad 2). In the early works, transport is still evoked as an expense (*De emptione*, III), but Aquinas progressively addresses it via a risk-based approach.

Mapping and Drawing Typologies of Risks: Towards a Dynamic Structure

A reading of his early writings on economic issues allows us to identify a set of risks and to map them text by text, depending on whether they are presented on the subject of usury, the activity of merchants, or the sale of goods on a forward basis (which is potentially related to the two former activities), or whether they use the expression "just price" to deal with situations of exchange. This then enables a set of risk typologies to be identified. Risks can then be classified, according to the economic analysis,

- by *activity* (loan, commercial exchange, limit cases of market exchange);
- by *dimension* (quantitative or qualitative); and
- by *type* (analysis risk—error in understanding the transaction; commercial risk—external risk imposed on the co-contractors; strategic risk—internal risk arising from the lack of information on the co-contractor's intention).

A broader or more panoramic reading allows us to develop two complementary typologies. These typologies are less immediately given and result from a conceptual elaboration based on a review of the Thomasian oeuvre as a whole. The validity of these typologies must therefore be verified by a retrospective check that they conform to the letter of the text.

The first step of this broader reading is to mobilise the Thomasian conceptual apparatus used in his philosophy and theology; inherited from both Aristotle and the Church Fathers, these are concepts that permeate his way of reasoning even if he does not always explicitly employ them in economic questions. The first concept Aquinas uses is that of analogy, which he deploys in theology to deal with divine names. The second concept is that of the sign and the thing, on which he builds his theology of the sacraments. The use of analogy and the sign is particularly evident in the Thomasian understanding of the notion of just price.

Analogy is what allows us to escape an equivocity according to which names would take on different meanings when they are applied to God and when they are applied to created realities, to the point that man would have no access to the meaning of a word applied to God and could say nothing about Him, and it also allows us to escape a univocity that would reduce this meaning to that known to men, which would undermine divine transcendence. The analogy of proportionality constitutes a middle way where what is said is right, but the reality described exceeds what is said. It therefore implies a relationship of conformity without identity. Thus, for example, one can use the adjective "wise" to speak of God's wisdom given that one knows what human wisdom is.

Aquinas refers to the concept of sign when he distinguishes, for a sacrament, (1) a first level of reality, the visible sign (*sacramentum tantum*), for example, for the Eucharist the bread and wine; (2) a second level of reality, that of the sacred thing which is at the same time sign of an ultimate reality (*res et sacramentum*), for example, the body and blood of Christ present under the species of bread and wine after the priest has said the words of consecration; and (3) a third level of reality, the ultimate sacred thing (*res tantum*), for example, the grace conferred by God on those who receive the sacrament. In the same way, with a few nuances, the just price is ultimately a price according to a justice pre-existing the exchange, but which is manifested, by reason of sign and by analogy, in the effective just price on the market, and in the just price in the singular exchange.

While the conceptual elaboration of Aquinas's work as a whole affords us a more microscopic view of the specific mechanisms he introduces, and so deepens our understanding of the notion of just price, it is also an opportunity for a more synoptic or macroscopic review of his works with an economic scope. Thus, in a second step, after having explored the notion of just price in detail, I will adopt a greater hermeneutical distance in order to assess Aquinas's own relationship with the risk that is present in the situations he describes. To this end, I can draw up a typology of the roles that these descriptions play, not only as regards the expression of risk, whether explicit or implicit, but also regarding the occurrence of this risk. Indeed, through its orientations, choices and formulations, Aquinas's analysis can itself engender risk for the agents involved. The typical example of risk arising from Aquinas's analysis is the risk of scarcity: for while

Aquinas recognises the necessity of supply, there are several indications that his primary concern lies more in the morality of exchange than with the necessity that supply be uninterrupted.

This gives us two complementary typologies:

- by *level* (depending on the level of understanding of the concept or activity: risk on trade can be licitness risk, condition risk or remuneration risk; risk on just price can relate to all three levels of reality of the just price, that is, risk on the price of justice, risk on the just price in the market, risk on the just price in the singular exchange);
- by *extension* (risks explicitly named by Aquinas, risks implicitly deducible from the situation described and risks induced by Aquinas's treatment of the situation).

On the basis of these typologies, we can draw up a dynamic structure of risks as they appear in the early works, starting with (1) the risks that occur upstream of the exchange, then (2) characterising the risks in the exchange, and then (3) identifying the new risks that are situated upstream of the exchange but only appear through the exchange.

It is worth noting that the first risk highlighted is the risk of analysis, that is, a risk upstream of the transaction which the expert incurs for all the agents concerned, since there is a risk that he could make an error in his understanding of the operation. In the Middle Ages, it was the canonist or theologian who, by misunderstanding the nature of a transaction, could make an erroneous moral and legal judgement that would be prejudicial to the agents; but more generally, this is a risk borne by any observer with political, legal, social or moral influence whose analysis of the transaction has an effect on the agents, for example in terms of reputation, status, gain or the conditions under which the activity is conducted. Thus, the risk of analysis, which is universal and yet remains an unrecognised dimension of the Thomasian work, is part of its innovative character. We may, next, note the risks within the operation. These risks are both quantitative and qualitative and can be assimilated to risks concerning the price level and the thing (*quid*), which controls the conditions of the exchange. Indeed, it is the thing, and not the intention of the agents, that determines the justice of its exchange: its price, as well as the qualitative conditions of the exchange, which include the status of the co-contractors; the day of the calendar, which must be appropriate for the trade; and the modalities of the transaction. This leads to a new risk upstream of the exchange, concerning the possibility and the nature of the exchange according to the good exchanged: can the thing be exchanged? And if so, according to what type of exchange ratio: a price according to a ratio between values, or a ratio involving another form of counterpart? A risk therefore arises as to the tradable nature of the thing.

To display the analytical contribution of Aquinas's early works to the economic understanding of risk, I first draw up a map of risks text by text (Chap. 2), dealing first with usury, monetary lending and forward selling; then the activity of merchants, the general conditions of the practice of the activity and the composition of the price; and finally the introduction of the concept of just price, through the plurality of exchange ratios and the limit cases of commercial exchange. From this, I then formulate a set of typologies and establish the dynamic structure of risk (Chap. 3), firstly through a classification according to the activity and the qualitative or quantitative dimension of the risk, then according to the type of risk (analysis risk, commercial risk or strategic risk), before proposing an elaboration by level of reality of the fair price and by extension (implicit risk, explicit risk, induced risk), and then presenting the dynamic structure of risk that these works suggest.

References

Primary Sources

Bernoulli, Jacob. 1713. *Ars conjectandi*. Basilae Impensis Thurnisiorum fratrum.

Giles of Lessines. 1875. *De usuris*, Thomas d'Aquin. *Opera Omnia*, t. 28. Paris: Vivès.

Robert of Courçon. 1902. In *De usura*, ed. Georges Lefèvre. Lille: Travaux et mémoires de l'Université de Lille.

Thomas Aquinas. 1892. *Summa theologiae*, Ia IIae, qq. 71–114, ed. Leonina, t. 7. Rome: Typographia polyglotta, S. C. de Propaganda Fide.

———. 1897. *Summa theologiae*, IIa IIae, qq. 52–122, ed. Leonina, t. 9. Rome: Typographia polyglotta S. C. de Propaganda Fide.

———. 1929–1947. *Scriptum super Sententiis*, 4 t. Paris: P. Lethielleux.

———. 1969. *Sententia libri Ethicorum*, ed. Leonina, t. 47. Rome: Commissio Leonina.

———. 1971. *Sententia libri Politicorum*, ed. Leonina, t. 48. Rome: Commissio Leonina.
———. 1974. *Expositio super Isaiam ad litteram*, ed. Leonina, t. 28. Rome: Santa Sabina.
———. 1979. *Opuscula III*, ed. Leonina, t. 42. Rome: Commission Leonina.
———. 1982. *Quaestiones disputatae de malo*, ed. Leonina, t. 23. Paris/Rome: Commissio Leonina—J. Vrin.
———. 1989. *Expositio libri posteriorum*, ed. Leonina, t. 1*2. Paris/Rome: Commissio Leonina—J. Vrin.
———. 1996. *Quaestiones de quolibet*, ed. Leonina, t. 25.2. Paris/Rome: Commissio Leonina—ed. du Cerf.
William of Auxerre. 1980–1987. *Summa aurea*. Paris/Grottaferrata: ed. du Centre national de la recherche scientifique/Editiones Collegii S. Bonaventurae ad Claras Aquas.
William of Tocco. 2005. *L'histoire de saint Thomas d'Aquin (Ystoria)*. Paris: Cerf.

Secondary References

Byrne, Edmund. 1968. *Probability and Opinion: A Study in the Medieval Presuppositions of Post Medieval Theories of Probability*. The Hague: Martinus Nijhoff.
Daston, Lorraine. 1988. *Classical Probability in the Enlightenment*. Princeton: Princeton University Press.
Ellul, Jacques. 2013. *Histoire des institutions. Le Moyen Âge*. Paris: Presses Universitaires de France.
Ernst, Wolfgang. 2016. The Legists' Doctrine on Money and the Law from the Eleventh to the Fifteenth Centuries. In *Money in the Western Legal Tradition*, ed. David Fox and Wolfgang Ernst, 110–135. Oxford: Oxford University Press.
Hacking, Ian. 2006. *The Emergence of Probability*. 2nd ed. Cambridge: Cambridge University Press.
Hirschfeld, Mary L. 2018. *Aquinas and the Market*. Cambridge: Harvard University Press.
Imbach, Ruedi, and Adriano Oliva. 2009. *La philosophie de Thomas d'Aquin*. Paris: Vrin.
Januard, Jean-Pierre. 1973. Agent économique. In *Les sciences de l'économie*, ed. André Vanoli and Jean-Pierre Januard, 18–19. Paris: Hachette.
Januard, Pierre. 2024. Probability, Prudence, Danger: Thomas Aquinas on the Building of the Lexicon of Risk. *Journal of the History of Economic Thought* 46 (3): 421–442.
Kimball, Miles S. 1990. Precautionary Saving in the Small and in the Large. *Econometrica* 58 (1): 53–73.

Knight, Frank H. 1921. *Risk, Uncertainty and Profit.* Boston/New York: Houghton Mifflin Company.
Le Goff, Jacques. [2010] 2019. *Le Moyen Âge et l'argent, essai d'anthropologie historique.* Paris: Perrin.
Oliva, Adriano. 2006. *Les débuts de l'enseignement de Thomas d'Aquin et sa conception de la Sacra doctrina.* Paris: Vrin.
Porro, Pasquale. 2015. *Thomas Aquinas. A Historical and Philosophical Profile.* Washington, DC: The Catholic University of America Press.
Savage, Leonard J. 1954. *The Foundation of Statistics.* New York: Wiley.
Schuessler, Rudolf. 2019. *The Debate on Probable Opinions in the Scholastic Tradition.* Leiden: Brill.
Synan, Edward A. 1988. St. Thomas Aquinas and the Profession of Arms. *Mediaeval Studies* 50: 404–437.
Torrell, Jean-Pierre. 2012. *Saint Thomas d'Aquin, l'homme et son œuvre.* Paris: Cerf.
———. 2015. *Initiation à Saint Thomas d'Aquin*, nouvelle édition. Paris: Cerf.
Tugwell, Simon. 1988. *Albert & Thomas.* New York: Paulist Press.
Weisheipl, James A. [1974] 1993. *Frère Thomas d'Aquin.* Paris: Cerf.
Yuengert, Andrew M. 2012. *Approximating Prudence.* New York: Palgrave Macmillan.

CHAPTER 2

Mapping Risk

Abstract Thomas Aquinas addresses various economic activities in a manner scattered throughout his works, with each activity presenting distinct risks for different agents. Analysing his texts individually allows for the construction of a risk map addressing interest-based lending, commercial exchange and, at the boundaries of the market, the determination of the just exchange ratio (price or stipend) based on the nature of the good exchanged. This approach enables the reconstruction of what might be considered a Thomasian analysis of economic risk. The list of risks revealed by this mapping shows that risk affects all operations and agents in multiple ways. In his analysis, centred on an objective approach to the exchanged object and the nature of the operation, Aquinas highlights qualitative aspects of risk that are strikingly contemporary. However, the emergence of probability calculation in the modern era has often led to their neglect.

Keywords Risk mapping • Usury • Just price • Risk • Exchange ratio • Probability • Danger • Prudence

Introduction

The early works of Thomas Aquinas allow us to draw up a map of risks, on which basis I can propose a classification and then an interpretation. The three early texts of direct economic significance (two questions from the

P. Januard, *Thomas Aquinas on Risk in Economic Activity*,
https://doi.org/10.1007/978-3-031-83825-5_2

Table 2.1 Structure of risk mapping

Reference	*Book*	*Text*
Risks on usury (RU)		
RUcs	*Commentary on the Sentences*	*In III Sent.*, d. 37, a. 6
RUde	*De emptione*	*De emptione*, I, II, III, IV
Risks on trade (RT)		
RTcs	*Commentary in the Sentences*	*In IV Sent.*, d. 16, q. 4, a. 2, qc. 3
RTde	*De emptione*	*De emptione*, III
Risks on exchange ratio (RE)		
Resi	*Super Isaiam*	*Super Isaiam*, 55, 1
Recs	*Commentary on the Sentences*	*In IV Sent.*, d. 25, q. 3, a. 1, qc. 1
		In IV Sent., d. 36, q. 1, a. 2

Commentary on the Sentences and *De emptione*) deal with four aspects of the activity of exchange: lending at interest, forward selling, the inclusion of expenses in the price and the contours of the activity of merchants. Each of these operations involves risks for the agents. In addition, three texts that are not strictly speaking economic but rather spiritual (*Commentary on the Book of Isaiah*) and theological (treatise on the *Commentary on the Sentences* on the Sacraments), in which Aquinas introduces the notion of a "just price", also show the risks that bear on the justice of the exchange ratio. All of these texts, scattered throughout the early works, thus offer a relatively detailed map of economic risks.

Risk mapping makes it possible to identify risks according to the economic activity concerned and the text in which they appear (Table 2.1):

Risks on Usury

Usury is dealt with in the early works from two angles: monetary lending at interest and forward selling. The interest-bearing loan will be developed at greater length in later works such as the *Summa theologiae*, but its initial treatment in the *Commentary on the Sentences*, characterised by a review of the positions of the authorities, the predecessors to whom Aquinas refers, brings to light a series of risks. The first risk is of a specific and singular nature, namely the risk of analysis. Aquinas points to the possibility of an error in his predecessors' understanding of the loan and of interest. This is not a risk incurred by the agents during the transaction, but a risk located upstream, which the expert makes the agents incur. By questioning the understanding of his predecessors—those who, as moralists, have decided on the morality and licitness of interest lending on the basis of their understanding of such lending and on the moral, legal and social reputation of borrowers and lenders—Aquinas suggests the possibility of an error of analysis on their part. This analysis risk is specific to the *Commentary on the Sentences*, which, as an early work, assigns an important place to the review of previous positions; it is not expressed explicitly by Aquinas afterwards and, since it is exogenous and does not belong to the exchange itself, is rarely taken into account in economic analysis. Yet it is nevertheless crucial, because, whatever the period, the situation of the agents is affected by the political, social, legal or moral recommendations of the expert according to his understanding of the situation that he analyses. Secondly, Aquinas addresses forward selling. This is a particular focus for development in the early works, with a short treatise dedicated to it, namely *De emptione*, whereas in the mature works, it will only constitute a particular case of usury. By conjoining lending and commercial exchange, *De emptione* allows the risk of usury to be considered as a risk weighing on the justice of the price. While the *Commentary on the Sentences* referred implicitly to a price risk, should the sum returned be not equal to the sum lent, *De emptione* takes up this risk explicitly through the notion of a just price. There is usury when the good is sold in time at a price that is not just because of time. The early works thus constitute a unique contribution concerning the risk that bears on usurious activity, and more broadly all economic activity: a risk of analysis and a risk of price.

Interest-Bearing Loans: The First Thomasian Approach to Economic Activity

Aquinas's first writing of direct economic significance, in the *Commentary on the Sentences* (*In III Sent.*, d. 37, a. 6), deals with usury: "Is it a sin to receive interest?" (Januard 2021). It introduces a novel feature into the *distinctio* focused on the Decalogue by including a specific and lengthy article on usury, along with six objections and their answers.[1] This is indicative of the importance Aquinas assigned to the question of usury.

The *sed contra* is moral, starting from the traditional Gospel verse calling on us to "lend without any hope of return [*date mutuum, nihil inde sperantes*]" (Luke 6:35). This verse is a classic reference point in mediaeval condemnations of usury: although it does not appear in Peter Lombard's writings, it is found at the beginning of the thirteenth century in Robert of Courçon's *De usura* (p. 5 and p. 19), and then in William of Auxerre's *Summa aurea*, III, XLVIII, c. 1, q. 1 and in Albert the Great's *In III Sent.*, d. 37, a. 13. It is cited by Gregory IX in his *Decretals* (1234) in a passage attributed to Urban III in 1186, which deals with sale on credit (*Decretales*, l. 5, t. 19, c. 10). Aquinas then turns to it regularly as a point of support: in addition to *In III Sent.*, d. 37, a. 6, s. c., it is found in other writings on usury (*S. T.*, IIa IIae, q. 78, a. 1, obj. 4; *De malo*, q. 14, a. 4, obj. 3), as well as in other places (*S. T.*, Ia IIae, q. 108, a. 3, ad 2; *Commentary on the Psalms*, 14, 5; *Catena aurea on St. Luke*, 6, 35). Finally, there would be two occurrences of the verse in the treatise on usury by Giles of Lessines (*De usuris*, III and XIV) written at the end of the thirteenth century.

The verse, in Latin, posits a tension between two notions: *mutuum*, which is understood as the loan stemming from Roman law, and *sperare*, waiting (Le Goff 1986, 23–24). Although it is understood and employed in the Middle Ages as an exhortation to lend without interest, the context given by Luke 6:27–35 and the lexicon employed may lead to a wide diversity of readings of the verse, and then to different hypotheses on the meaning of understanding put forward by mediaeval thinkers. The whole passage is focused on love and gift: "Give to everyone who asks you, and do not ask for your property back from someone who takes it" (Luke 6:30). And then the Gospel says: "and if you lend (*mutuum dederitis*) to

[1] The *Commentary on the Sentences* is articulated in books, distinctions (*distinctio*), questions and articles. The *Summa theologiae* simplifies the outline by removing the distinctions and tightening up the articles for pedagogical purposes. Each article focuses on answering a question. It is made up of a series of objections, which are generally not false, but which serve as points of support to be surpassed or clarified. Next comes the *sed contra* (on the contrary), which gives the key to Aquinas's position, usually drawing from a biblical, patristic or philosophical quotation, and then the *respondeo* (answer, or main part of the article), which presents the author's thesis, often by a process of distinction that allows the question to be approached from different angles in a nuanced manner. Finally, there are the replies to the objections, which are term-by-term responses.

those from whom you hope to receive, what is your grace? Even sinners lend (*foenerantur*) to sinners to get back the equivalent (*aequalia*)" (Luke 6:34). The *Vulgate* uses a twofold Latin lexicon, lending as a "*mutuum*" and lending as a "*fenus*", in order to translate into Latin the Greek verb δανίζω which means "to lend money at interest", as has been pointed out by Ege (2014, 396). The *Vulgate* thus makes a primary hermeneutic distinction: the righteous person lends without interest (*mutuum*), whereas the sinner lends at interest (*fenus*).

The second issue of vocabulary in Luke 6:34 concerns the equivalent (*aequalia*), translating the Greek τὰ ἴσα (equivalents), expected by sinners. This equivalent may have many different meanings: it may mean the sum lent including interest, the sum lent without interest, the repayment of the loan, the granting of an equivalent service in exchange, or the granting of an equivalent loan in return (Bovon 1991, 311; Schürmann 1983, 577–578). The meaning given to this "equivalent" guides the general understanding of the passage. It may be a denunciation of the expectation of interest or of the reciprocity of lending practised by sinners. This would argue in favour of an understanding of the following verse as mediaeval authors did: we should lend without expecting interest or a loan in return.

However, the original meaning of "equivalent" and the vagueness that Luke, who is usually precise, may employ, could point towards a denunciation of any idea of reciprocity or return, with or without interest. This would be consistent with the call to gift in Luke 6:30 and would lead to a more radical interpretation of Luke 6:35 than that offered by mediaeval thinkers: "to lend, without expecting anything in return" would mean lending without expecting anything, not even the repayment of the capital. The *Vulgate*'s choice of the expression "*date mutuum*" here, excluding the idea of interest, unlike the Greek imperative δανίζετε it translates, would place the emphasis on the very idea of lending and reciprocity. In this case, the mediaeval thinkers' interpretation would soften the paradoxical nature of the *Vulgate*'s expression.[2]

[2] We must add to the lexical complexity of the passage that, while the *Vulgate* offers a version of the verse that may be paradoxical but is coherent, the Greek presents an additional difficulty. The verb ἀπελπίζω does not mean "to hope for a return" but "to despair". This has led modern commentators either to look for ways of interpreting the verse in this sense, or to consider that it was a confusion with ἐπελπίζω, which means "to put one's hope in", or a rare form with the prefix ἀπό (coming from) to mean "to hope in return", as the *Vulgate* and John Chrysostom do (Bovon 1991, 311–312).

However, it is necessary to continue the analysis in order to better understand the process of translation of δανίζετε by *date mutuum*. By choosing the expression "*date mutuum*", the Latin translators of the Greek text thus associate the *mutuum* with a loan which, according to the Greek, is usually made at interest. Two hypotheses then arise concerning the meaning of the term *mutuum* for mediaeval authors: either the translators of the Greek suppressed the notion of interest by choosing the term *mutuum* which for them does not evoke interest, or else the term *mutuum* does indeed contain the possibility of interest. The work of the Fathers and the mediaeval theologians would then be aimed at explicating a new conception of the *mutuum* without interest.

The general meaning of *mutuum* in Latin literature is first of all lending among friends,[3] and then lending in the broad sense, whether in money or in kind, without specifying interest (unlike δανίζετε), but nevertheless with a notion of reciprocity or mutuality: the equivalent must be returned (Ege 2014, 393).[4] The term *fenus*[5] is used to refer to interest, and by extension to interest-bearing loans: this term is thus employed to emphasise the specific nature of such loans and makes it possible to distinguish interest from capital, *sors* (Ernout and Meillet 2001, 225, 426, 637). However, the terminology remains relatively imprecise.[6]

[3] For Plautus (d. 184 BC), one of the first great Latin authors, the loans were made to family or friends and carried no interest, as indicated by all the occurrences noted by Feuvrier-Prévotat (1993). However, we see the emergence of the profession of usurers (*danista*) and bankers (*argentarii*), which were not mentioned in the Greek comedies we know of (Feuvrier-Prévotat 1993, 143). Pre-Ciceronian authors usually reserve *mutuum* for an interest-free loan and call *fenus* interest (Nadjo 1989, 233–307).

[4] In Cicero (d. 43 BC), for example, there is a *mutuum* in kind without mention of interest (or free of charge): "wheat is lent to two cities in Sicily (*mutuum frumentum dedit*)" (Cicero, *On the Agrarian Law*, II, XXX, 83).

[5] The two forms, *fenus* and *fenum*, the product of the meadow, retain different meanings, although the Romans understood the relationship between the two terms (Ernout and Meillet 2001, 225). The Romans, like Festus and Varro, also associated *fenus* with *fetus*, progeny, because deniers generate deniers (du Passage 1946, col. 2321).

[6] In Cicero's view, *fenus* can refer to income in a sense close to interest, for which the term used can be *usura*, but without any pejorative connotation, suggesting on the contrary generosity: "Indeed, the farmers have an open account with the land, which never pushes back their domination and never makes without interest [*sine usura reddit*] what it has received, but gives an income sometimes small, most often considerable (*plerumque majorum* cum *fenore*)" (Cicero, *Cato the Elder*, XV, 51). The term *fenus* is used to denounce an interest-bearing loan that is usurious: "He received an interest of two per cent per month (*binis centesimis feneratus*); then, there are very many cities where he paid absolutely nothing for the wheat" (Cicero, *Second Pleading against Verres*, III, LXX, 165).

In Roman law,[7] particularly under Justinian's rule, the *mutuum* was initially a consumer loan contract free of interest,[8] to which may be added a *stipulatio*, an appendix that sets out what the borrower must give in addition to returning what has been borrowed.[9] The borrower becomes the owner of the borrowed sum, contrary to the three other types of real contracts: the commodate, the deposit (*depositum*) and the pledge (*pignus*). The *fenus nauticum* is thus a variant derogating from the interest of the *mutuum* justified by the specific nature of the sea trade but which is part of the common law.[10] More generally, the reasons for a *stipulatio* are very varied, and interest is only one of the possible specifications. In addition, in the thirteenth century, there were many variants of interest *stipulatio*, which can be grouped into two categories: fixed term or at the will of the creditor. This was the case, for example, in Flanders (Wyffels 1991, 855). The extrinsic titles attached to the loan may include: *lucrum cessans*, to cover the opportunity cost of the loan, which prevents the lender from doing other business; *damnum emergens*, if the lender is himself forced to borrow at interest (in particular to take out a consumer loan) because of the loan; and *poena conventionalis*, a penalty for late payment for a loan that was originally free (although this is disguised interest when this "delay" is agreed in advance). The clauses and titles intended to justify the interest are

[7] On the rediscovery of Roman law in the Middle Ages, see in particular Lapidus (1987, 1098–1099).

[8] Since the loan is initially a consumer loan, this explains the difference in bargaining power between borrower and lender (Chaplygina and Lapidus 2016, 32; 2022).

[9] On the common practice of attaching to the *mutuum*, which normally carries no interest, a stipulation that envisages some interest, see Giliberti (1999, 169); Cimma (1984). Andreau, by noting on the one hand the practice of attaching a stipulation of interest to *the mutuum* (2000, 152), and by presenting *mutuum* and *fenus* as two alternatives depending on whether there is interest or not (1987, 433), echoes the lexical diversity of Latin authors, although *fenus* is usually designated as a *mutuum* with *stipulatio* (du Passage 1946, col. 2321).

[10] Lapidus (1991) and Chaplygina and Lapidus (2016, 39), in breaking down the *fenus nauticum* into two stages, bring it closer to the *societas* and see it as a loan only in name. After the maritime risk, there remains a risk of loss during the sale, which was not taken into account in the contract. The lender continues to bear the risk, since it is his money that has been invested in the transaction. He therefore becomes a shareholder of the commercial transaction, as it were.

thus based on the expression of a risk.[11] We may note, however, that until the sixteenth century, the licit forms of credit, under the legal aspects of investment or *locatio*, were more frequent than *stipulatio* (Mélitz 1971, 475 and 484–485). Foreign exchange was also an alternative form of usury (De Roover 1946, 118). De Roover (1953, 28–29) thus shows that foreign exchange contracts (*mutuo nomine cambi*) were common in Genoa in the twelfth century, but that the term *mutuum* was quickly abolished so as not to fall foul of the condemnation of usury, and that the transaction was presented as a purchase and sale (*emptio-venditio*). Ege (2014, 392) thus observes that usury could never be prevented and was the subject of multiple "escape attempts", as he puts it, of two types: circumvention by a legal covering of the shareholder type, and the stipulation of clauses of interest in the *mutuum* (Chaplygina and Lapidus 2016, 37; 2022).

Halfway between the two previously formulated hypotheses for translation (a *mutuum* with or without the possibility of interest), the history of Roman law invites us to see in the translation of δανίζετε by *mutuum* an enlargement, with a shift in meaning towards a "rather" interest-free loan, and then a new shift under the mediaeval theologians back towards the original meaning of a *mutuum* clearly without interest, thus departing from the Greek term and the paradox it introduced. Mediaeval authors adopted the *mutuum* of Roman law as the prototypical form of lending (Mélitz 1971, 478), but they did not immediately rely on it to condemn usury. Thus, Gratian's *Decree* (1140) does not explicitly refer to the definition of the *mutuum* in its argument against usury. The ambiguity or polysemy of the *mutuum* can be compared to the expression "loan *ad maniam*" or "*a manaie*", used in the thirteenth century, originally thought of and understood as a free loan, a deposit, but which was practiced by the cities of Flanders with an interest of about 10% and which appears under the heading *usura* in their accounts (Wyffels 1991, 859–862).[12]

[11] On extrinsic titles, see McLaughlin (1939, 125–147); du Passage (1946, col. 2361 and 2364); Noonan (1957, 105–132); Mélitz (1971, 475 and 484–485); Lapidus (1987, 1103–1108); Lapidus (1991); Lapidus (1992, 47–49); Lapidus (2021); Wyffels (1991, 853); Langholm (1998, 74–76); Munro (2003, 511–512); Franks (2009, 70–83); Rajapakse (2010, 212–219); Todeschini (2012, 128); Burke (2014, 111–113); Ege (2014, 403); Monsalve (2014b, 231–232); Chaplygina and Lapidus (2016, 35–37); Chaplygina and Lapidus (2022); Januard (2021, 607 and 628–629).

[12] In the twelfth and thirteenth centuries, European cities regularly needed to resort to borrowing, sometimes forced, sometimes free, as Munro (2003) shows for Genoa and Venice (514–515), and for Northern Europe through *rente* contracts (518).

However, one observes in Robert of Courçon's *De usura*, for example, a desire to restore an evangelical meaning to the *mutuum* by seizing upon Luke 6:35 and returning to the primary and restrictive meaning, void of any *stipulatio*. It is not the level of the interest rate nor the reason for the loan that determines a loan to be usury, but the very fact of giving an interest-bearing loan (De Roover 1971, 78), at least in the *mutuum* analysis framework. While Gratian does not make this point explicitly, Robert goes on to insist on the importance of the change of ownership, relying on the supposed etymology of *mutuum*, playing on *meum-tuum*: "what is mine becomes yours or conversely (*de meo fit tuum vel e converso*)" (*De usura*, p. 14)—by contrast, the agreed etymology today is that the word is a form derived from *muto*, to move, to change (Ernout and Meillet 2001, 426). In the *Decretals* of 1234, Gregory IX takes up the notion of *mutuum* as a transfer of ownership that prohibits interest, but the expressions using the term remain rare and allusive: "*mutuam pecuniam*" in *Decretals*, l. 5, t. 19, c. 10; "*certam mutuans pecuniae quantitam*" in c. 19, *Decretal Naviganti*. We must, therefore, ascertain whether Aquinas, by the choice of Luke 6:35 in the *sed contra*, first of all, fits into the mediaeval narrowing of the sense of *mutuum* initiated by the previous users of this verse, or whether he intends to return to the broader sense of Roman law.

In the *respondeo*, which constitutes the heart of the expression of his thought, Aquinas takes up the question by making reference to three arguments against usury inherited from the authorities. The first risk that appears, specific in its nature, is a risk of analysis of the loan at interest. A series of clues suggests that he is distancing himself from the way in which his predecessors understood the interest-bearing loan and justified its prohibition. It is not uncommon for Aquinas to take a position in relation to these authorities, but it is usually in a more diffuse manner, whereas here, his response consists of a critical review of earlier positions. His consideration, at the very heart of his own analysis of an economic activity, of a risk of error in the understanding of this operation, deserves particular attention. For this possibility of an error in analysis does indeed lie at the heart of Aquinas's thought, and though he will not explicitly take it up again in his later works, this is in large part because those works are dedicated to presenting more of his own thought. Moreover, Aquinas here raises an issue of which there is little trace in entirety of the history of economic thought. This internal consideration of the risk of error is therefore of major epistemological interest both because of its uniqueness and because of the universal character of this risk. Moreover, the authorities to whom he refers, although they remain anonymous in the text, are the theologians and canonists who were the experts of their time, charged with guiding the moral, social, legal and political treatment of the activity of interest lending and the agents who engage in it. Beyond the purely intellectual risk of an error in analysis, therefore, Aquinas also highlights an actual risk for the agents concerned. This concerns not only the lender and the borrower, to whom this text of the *Commentary on the Sentences* refers, but more generally the prince and the population as a whole, as will be shown later in the *Letter to the Duchess of Brabant*, devoted to the question of what the prince should do with the taxes levied on usurious gains and whether their social redistribution is permissible.

The risk of analysis appears in several ways. First, Aquinas introduces the arguments of the authorities in general terms: "But divers [persons] give divers reasons [*sed diversi diversas rationes assignant*]". The authorities are not named, and the term *diversi/diversas* originally carries an idea of opposition, implying here that the arguments point at least in various, if not opposing, directions. Aquinas does not question the general position, which he stresses is unanimous—"All commonly say that usury is a mortal sin"—but the introduction to the argument suggests some critical distance. Aquinas then gives the first reason, which concerns the definition of money (*pecunia*), which, here, "is not destroyed by use [*non deterioratur ex usu*]" (*In III Sent.*, d. 37, a. 6, resp.). This non-deterioration is posited as specific to money, and as justifying that there is no surplus paid to the lender; but Aquinas notes the fragility of the argument, since some goods, such as a house, do not deteriorate either. He does not pursue the argument further, but returns to it in the *Summa theologiae* (*S. T.*, IIa IIae, q. 78, a. 1, resp.) by arguing that the principal use of money is to be consumed (*ad consummendas faciendas*). He therefore concludes: "That is why others give other reasons" (*In III Sent.*, d. 37, a. 6, resp.). The risk of error on the part of the authorities is thus present from the very first argument stated.

The first indication of Aquinas's distancing himself from the authorities is therefore the fact that he presents their arguments in an anonymous and general form. The second indication is that he judges the first argument to be weak because it does not fit economic reality: what is presented as a specific quality of money, its non-deterioration in the course of use, is not unique to it, being also the case for other goods such as houses, which are nevertheless subject to rent. The third clue is the use of the notion of probability, here applied to the second argument. Probability implicitly involves the possibility of an event not being realised or of an argument not being verified.

Aquinas presents the second and most common argument, the understanding of a money loan as a *mutuum*: "when money is lent, property is transferred [*quando pecunia mutuatur, transfertur dominum*]", and "nothing is received in exchange"; he concludes: "This reason is considered to be quite probable [*et haec ratio satis probabilis videtur*]" (*In III Sent.*, d. 37, a. 6, resp.). From the mediaeval and Thomasian use of the terms *satis* and *probabilis*, the expression *satis probabilis* may be understood here as an absence of certainty, or even as a doubt (Januard 2021, 611–621; Januard 2024a, 425–430). This understanding is open to debate. Indeed, *satis* has an ambivalent connotation. The adverb can evoke sufficiency (Quicherat 1893, 999), particularly as a prefix (Gardin-Dumesnil 1788, 560), and we could therefore understand *satis* as "very much". This would reinforce the understanding of *probabilis* as "credible", as the expression of a position held to be true (for a comprehensive analysis, see Schuessler 2019, 22–59). This would then be consistent with the fact that Aquinas seems to take up the argument in the rest of the article without expressing any doubt (*In III Sent.*, d. 37, a. 6, ad 5).

On the contrary, there are a number of indications that we are expressing a doubt. The adverb "*satis*" can also evoke incompleteness (Blaise 1954, 740; Blaise 1975, 820; Ernout and Meillet 2001, 596). In this case, it means "rather". A middle way would consist in translating it as "enough" or "almost", but it does not seem right to adopt such a positive connotation according to all elements. Moreover, probability, while expressing something that is credible, is not yet a "degree of certainty [*gradus certitudinis*]" as it is for Jacob Bernoulli in 1713 in his *Ars conjectandi* (IV, 1, p. 211 and IV, 4, p. 225) with the advent of the calculus of probabilities, that is very useful to address economic matters (Bréban and Lapidus 2019, 158), as Bernoulli does. For Aquinas, following Aristotle, what is probable is not certain (Byrne 1968; Daston 1988; Hacking 2006). These are two different orders of knowledge, which is either apodictic (universal and absolute truth) by way of demonstration, or persuasive, by way of a set of opinions and arguments (Daston 1988, 37–38). This distinction includes the notion of faith, *fides*, developed by Aquinas (*S. T.*, IIa IIae, q. 2, a. 1, resp.) to describe a form of assent to an existent which is non-evident and the knowledge thereof therefore a matter of probability (Wirth 1983, 21–22, Schuessler 2019, 30–36). Aquinas presents the two distinct ways of reasoning, apodictic and persuasive, at the beginning of his *Commentary* on Aristotle's *Posterior Analytics* (*In Post.*, I, 1, l. 65–74). He thus takes up Aristotle's distinction, for whom the plausible or probable characterises "not what is always, but what is often" (Aristotle, *Rhetoric*, II, 1402b20–21. See also I, 1357a24–35). Thus, the use of *satis probabilis* is an expression of a risk of error. In addition, the expression *haec ratio* leaves ambiguity as to what this judgement applies to: whether the loan is a transfer of property or whether this transfer of property prevents a surplus. Aquinas then concludes, without making a judgement on it, with the third argument, which holds that money has no utility of its own but serves to measure the utility of other goods.

Thus, it can be seen that a salient feature of Aquinas's first economic writing is that, out of the three reasons commonly given to explain the usury mechanism and justify its prohibition, he maintains that the first is fragile and the second is not certain but only fairly probable. Moreover, as we have seen, the authorities are not mentioned by name and appear only in general terms. And to this, another clue should be added: when Aquinas mentions several arguments in his writing, it is usually the case that he considers none of them to be decisive.

The risk of analysis is thus expressed by Aquinas via four signs that he distances himself from his predecessors' understanding of the money loan:

1. A general and anonymous presentation of their arguments.
2. His emphasis that the arguments are an inadequate account of the economic reality concerning the alleged unique nature of money.
3. The understanding of loan as *mutuum* as of only probable validity.
4. The succession of three arguments, one of which is contested, one of which does not seem to be entirely satisfactory and a third which is presented very quickly.

We can conclude that Aquinas's thinking on economic matters thus opens under the auspices of doubt.

This first text also identifies the nature of the risk attached to interest-bearing loans by showing to what type of activity it relates and sheds new light on the later presentation of economic issues in the *Summa theologiae* and other writings. For example, a distinction is usually made between q. 77 and 78, the former dealing with trade and the latter with lending, each of which highlights a different sin, fraud in case of trade (*S. T.*, IIa IIae, q. 77), usury in case of lending (*S. T.*, IIa IIae, q. 78); and indeed, in his other writings Aquinas treats of these two operations in distinct places.

However, the prologue to q. 77 is a prologue to both questions, 77 and 78, and it brings the two operations under the same heading, "voluntary exchanges [*voluntarias commutationes*]" (*S. T.*, IIa IIae, q. 77, prol.). And this unification seems to have been initiated by the first text with an economic scope, *In III Sent.*, d. 37, a. 6, especially given that we know that in a second stage, in *De emptione*, Aquinas would address the sale of futures, an activity which combines the two operations.

In this first text, usury is presented as a commercial exchange with a price that is not fair: "receiving more money for [a lesser sum] [*accipere majorem pecuniam pro minori*] [...] modifies the measure in receiving and giving, which clearly constitutes an iniquity" (*In III Sent.*, d. 37, a. 6, resp.). In other words, "the benefit of the loan [*beneficium mutui*] is not greater than the sum exchanged [*pecunia mutata*]" (*In III Sent.*, d. 37, a. 6, ad 2). The presence of an interest breaks the equality of thing to thing that ensures the just price according to commutative justice (*S. T.*, IIa IIae, q. 77, a. 1, ad 3). The loan is a transfer of property and is therefore similar to a sale, the price of which is the sum lent. This approach to lending as a commercial exchange will be confirmed in the *Summa theologiae*, where question 78 on usury is treated within the framework of commutative justice, which governs an exchange with a price that is an equality of thing to thing, which is the exchange ratio that ensures this justice.

Secondly, this early Thomasian article on usury presents two principles that would structure his analysis, although here succinctly expressed: firstly, the same person who incurs the risk receives the profit, which is translated in terms of ownership, since here the risk falls to the owner: "The very fact that the ownership of money is transferred is the reason why I must receive or expect nothing for its use as if it were due to me" (*In III Sent.*, d. 37, a. 6, ad 5). Secondly, each person must assume his own risk and cannot pass it on to others: "Whatever usefully comes to him to whom I have granted a loan, beyond the measure of the loan according to the money lent, comes from the efforts [*industria*] of him who has wisely used the money. I must not sell him his efforts, just as I must not receive less because of his stupidity" (*In III Sent.*, d. 37, a. 6, ad 4). These two principles, the risk/profit pairing expressed in terms of the risk/ownership pairing and the risk/responsibility pairing, go beyond the framework of usury and form the common basis for the analysis of voluntary exchanges as a whole. In the commercial exchange, each must manage his own risk: the seller must not make imprudent expenditures and transfer the risks to his client by including them in the price (*De emptione*, III), and the buyer must be vigilant about the condition of what he buys and it is up to him to detect visible defects in the good (*S. T.*, IIa IIae, q. 77, a. 3).

Aquinas thus lays the foundations of his analysis of risk in his very first economic text:

1. The first risk is located upstream of the operation; it is a risk of understanding the operation.
2. The risk in the transaction is a price risk, that is, a risk that the counterpart is not of equal value to the thing exchanged, thus affecting commutative justice, and a risk about the nature of the thing (in this case, money), which determines its exchangeability and the conditions of this exchange.
3. The risk that the one who receives the profit is not the one who incurs the risk of loss.

This leads to some risks for agents:[13]

RUcs1: A reputational risk for the observer, if his analysis is wrong.

RUcs2: A reputational risk for the agent who is wrongly deemed to be a usurer because of the observer's erroneous analysis.

RUcs3: A risk to the borrower if the interest loan was wrongly authorised.

RUcs4: A risk to all agents, lenders and borrowers, who would have an interest in usury if it is wrongly prohibited.

RUcs5: A strategic risk for the lender that the borrower will take advantage of the risk of analytical error to make him look like a usurer.

RUcs6: A strategic risk for the borrower that the usurer will take advantage of the risk of analytical error to make his usurious activity look licit.

The text of the *Commentary on the Sentences* on usury remains relatively brief and allusive, but the issue of usury is then developed further, notably in the *Letter to the Duchess of Brabant* (*Ad ducissam Brabantiae*), *De malo* (q. 13, a. 4), the *Quodlibetal Questions* (*III Quodl.*, q. 7, a. 2) and the *Summa theologiae* (IIa IIae, q. 78). In addition, the *Commentary on the Sentences* addresses the specific issue of money lending.

We note, however, that Aquinas here lays a triple foundation. First, he sets the basis for his later understanding of usury, which comes about through a combination of an approach through ownership (*mutuum*) and

[13] Risks on usury in the *Commentary on the Sentences, III Sent.*, d. 37, a. 6, numbered "RUcs".

through the nature of money. Moreover, by comparing the sum lent and the sum returned, he implicitly addresses the justice of lending through the notion of the exchange ratio, and thus lays the groundwork for a price of lending. If here the ratio is one to one, this opens the way to Aquinas's progressive opening to extrinsic titles, which would in certain cases allow this ratio to be corrected externally, so that the exchange is just (compensation for the damage caused by the deprivation of the sum (*damnum emergens*) in *S. T.*, IIa IIae, q. 78, a. 2, ad 1 and for a delay in repayment (*poena conventionalis*), in *De malo*, q. 13, a. 4, ad 14). Secondly, this text lays down the foundations of Thomasian economic thought more broadly considered, which will also apply to commercial exchange: attention to the price and the thing exchanged, and the responsibility of each agent in the face of the risk he must assume. Finally, we see that this early text, however brief and allusive, makes a decisive epistemological move that will be implicit in all of Aquinas's later work, and that still strikes the reader today by its originality: integrating into the very heart of the analysis of the economic operation a risk of error in the understanding of this operation.

Forward Buying and Selling: Usury as Price Injustice

A few years after the *Commentary on the Sentences*, written in Paris, Aquinas returned to Italy and wrote *De emptione et venditione ad tempus*, which O'Rahilly (1928) helped to bring to the attention of English-speaking readers. *De emptione* did not appear in the catalogues of Aquinas's works until the fourteenth century, and its attribution was considered doubtful until the beginning of the twentieth century when Pierre Mandonnet (1910, 116–120) established its authenticity and dated it to 1262; this date was confirmed, with greater caution, by the Commissio Leonina in the critical edition published almost 70 years later (Dondaine 1979, 384). *De emptione* was written during Aquinas's stay in Orvieto (1261–1265) as a conventual lecturer (Torrell 2015, 160–162 and 168–170; Imbach and Oliva 2009, 21; Porro 2015, 441). The text therefore precedes the mature economic writings by about ten years and would thus appear to be an intermediate work, roughly halfway between the *Commentary on the Sentences* and the subsequent writings, which therefore benefit from the more technical reflections of this short treatise. The addressee would be friar James of Viterbo, who seems to have solicited this text from Aquinas (Dondaine 1979, 384–385).

Mandonnet gives details of Aquinas's appointment and fills in the context. James was a lecturer in the convent of Florence, a city where the draper's trade and associated industry had been developing rapidly since the turn of the century:

> As a professor in the most famous convent in the city, [James] like his confreres often had to give solutions to cases of conscience, which were made all the more difficult by the intense business life in Florence. (Mandonnet 1910, 119)

Aquinas therefore examines the potentially usurious situation of Italian merchants who come from Tuscany to sell their cloth at the Lagny fair, near Paris, and who are accustomed to settling the sale three months later, in particular to allow time to ship the goods. Aquinas excludes from the outset the case of usurious intent. He limits himself to the objective and observable justice of the exchange:

> Assuming that the custom of postponing settlement [*de dilatione solutionis*] for three months, as proposed, is for the common good of merchants [*ad commune bonum mercatorum*], namely, for the shipment of their goods, and that it was not introduced by the deception of usury, it seems that a distinction must be made. (*De emptione*, 1)

Aquinas thus addresses different cases that may occur in forward selling. This short treatise, barely two pages and 80 lines long in the Leonine edition, was slow to spread and for a long time remained unknown. The editors of the Commissio Leonina justified the lack of initial diffusion of this text by its lack of originality. The forward sale discussed here would only be a particular case of usury, and "the doctrine is that of the *S. T.*, IIa IIae (q. 78, a. 2, ad 6), condensed into this simple norm: there is usury when one sells the period of payment" (Dondaine 1979, 385). Mandonnet, for his part, seemed to afford the treatise more originality, saying that Aquinas was nowhere else so "in touch with the realities of everyday life and the economic concerns of his time" (Mandonnet 1910, 119).

Yet *De emptione* seems much more original and important than has been perceived. On the one hand, in fact, the sale of goods on a forward basis is a matter of both usury and trade. It is not a particular case but a case of usury much more broadly understood, which is thus not reduced to the money loan. By devoting a treatise to the forward sale of goods, and treating the two aspects of the operation, commercial and usurious, in a unified way, Aquinas here tends to confirm the unified approach to economic activity of which the *Commentary on the Sentences* already gave some indications in *In III Sent.*, d. 37, a. 6. On the other hand, for the first time in his economic works, Aquinas introduces the notion of just price, which he had already used three times in economic examples or metaphors in his theological treatises (*Super Isaiam*, 55, 1; *In IV Sent.*, d. 25, q. 3, a. 1, qc. 1 and *In IV Sent.*, d. 36, q. 1, a. 2). This notion was already implicit, but not explicitly formulated, in the treatment of usury in *In III Sent.*, d. 37, a. 6, and takes a central place in Thomasian thought because the price reduces the risk of injustice in the exchange by constituting a visible and objective criterion of justice. In the case of forward sales, the risk weighing on the fair price is an usurious risk. Usury occurs if one sells for more than the fair price because a surcharge is imposed "for the expectation [*propter expectationem*]"; in other words, one receives more than the sum due "because of the delay in time [*propter temporis dilationem*]" (*De emptione*, I).

The risk of being in a situation of usury may change in the course of the exchange (Januard 2022d). If the price that was set for a forward payment was fair and the buyer asks for a discount for an earlier payment, then he is the one who is in a situation of usury: "on the part of the one who gives less by paying more quickly, there seems to be a form of usury [*aliquis modus usurae*], since he sells time [*cum spatium temporis vendat*]" (*De emptione*, I). It is here, rather than in *In III Sent.*, d. 37, a. 6, that Aquinas introduces the notion of time, but on the one hand, without considering that the temporal preference for the present is a source of increase in the value of the good, whether it is money in the case of a loan or cloth in the case of a forward sale; and on the other hand without considering time as a source of risk for the lender. Indeed, there is a transfer of ownership, so the risk falls to the borrower, and Aquinas never considers the risk of absolute default in repayment, but simply, in late writings like *De malo*, a risk of delay in payment (*De malo*, q. 13, a. 4, ad 14).

The usurious risk is thus universalised. By looking at the course of the transaction, Aquinas does not confine himself to a pre-established determination of the usurious status of the agents. He can thus note the possibility for everyone, buyer or seller, to be a usurer or a victim of usury. This could be seen as a first emancipation from the social reputation of the usurer-lender and the merchant seller. Indeed, merchants constituted a new social group that had rapidly grown rich (Le Goff [2010] 2019,

121–231). They increasingly came to exercise economic and social domination (Le Goff [1956] 2001, 41–67), and were suspected of practicing usury dressed up as commerce (McLaughlin 1939, 75–95 and 1940; De Roover 1953, 28–29; Ege 2014, 392; Feller 2020, 59–61). However, the rest of *De emptione* shows that the moral focus is unilaterally on the merchant, and the setting of *De emptione* is the Lagny fair, where sellers and buyers are professional merchants. It is not until ten years later in the *Summa theologiae* that Aquinas's view is universalised to all agents, regardless of their social status. However, we can see here a first universalisation of risk, since the behaviour of the buyer-borrower can lead to usurious prejudice for the seller-lender.

Two risks can be perceived in the setting of the just price as Aquinas presents it. The first risk concerns the approximation of the just price. Indeed, the case of the buyer who pays less than expected by paying before the term allows Aquinas to introduce the notion of estimation, since the buyer buys "less than the just estimation [*justa aestimatione*]" (*De emptione*, I). Aquinas does not specify the meaning of the term "*aestimatio*" here, but his other use of the term in the context of price, ten years later in *S. T.*, IIa IIae, q. 77, a. 1, ad 1 includes a notion of approximation, which may shed light on this first usage. The just price is not determined with precision (*non est punctualiter determinatum*) but by an estimation (*in quadam aestimatione*) which justifies "a slight increase or decrease [*modica additivo vel minutio*]" in the price (*S. T.*, IIa IIae, q. 77, a. 1, ad 1). Although this does not seem to affect the equality of justice, Aquinas nevertheless foresees that it may give rise to compensation if the prejudice is significant. It has been shown that the just price reduces transaction costs because, in this respect, the price is given and does not require negotiation (Friedman 1980). But the estimation remains a source of a risk of error in the precise assessment of the just price which may harm one of the parties. This sheds light on the role of the market in setting the just price. The market is not the place where the just price is set, but it is the place where an estimate of the just price is found by approximation.

The notion of estimation as an approximation sheds light on the role of the market in determining the just price, which is the most debated topic among historians of Thomasian economic thought during the twentieth century, especially since this debate is rooted in *De emptione*. Indeed, Aquinas says that usury occurs when merchants "sell cloth for more than it is worth in the common market [*plus vendant pannos quam valeant secundum communem forum*]" (*De emptione*, III). Does the market establish the just price, or is it simply the place where this just price manifests itself? Does Aquinas present other instances of determining the just price in his work? A first line, followed for example by Tawney ([1926] 1948, 41), consisted in approaching the just price from the point of view of the costs of production by relying on the *Commentary* on Aristotle's *Nicomachean Ethics*: the just price that allows for exchange must ensure an equality of the costs of production "in labour and in expenses [*in labore et expensis*]" (*Ethicorum*, V, 9, n°3). A second line of thought has consisted, on the contrary, in granting this active role to the market by hardening the Thomasian expression a little by using the translation "according to the market price [*d'après le cours du marché*]" (De Roover 1971, 59) and by rendering the corresponding expression in Albert the Great, "*secundum aestimationem fori*" (Albert the Great, *In IV Sent.*, d. 16, a. 46), as "estimation *of* the market" (De Roover 1958, 422).[14] Moreover, the expression "market price" is regularly used to refer to the Thomasian or scholastic just price (De Roover 1958, 422; 39 times in Hollander 1965; regularly used in Monsalve 2014a when distinguishing between the cooperative scholastic market price and the competitive liberal market price). Some authors consider reconciling the two approaches with a market price that would fluctuate around the price derived from production costs (Hollander 1965).

The difficulty in attributing an active role to the market stems firstly from its anachronistic nature. The distinction that Steven Kaplan proposes when addressing the modern era between *marketplace* and *market principle* (Kaplan 1984, 25–29) is fully relevant here. On the one hand, the mediaeval market is a physical place, a *forum*, where people buy and sell, not a conceptual reality describing the conditions of exchange of a good (in the sense of the market for such and such a good); on the other hand, for Aquinas, the market is the place where exchange takes place at a certain price, which may be just, but it is not an active, price-producing conceptual space where the confrontation of supply and demand, represented by two curves that cross, would allow the fixing of a price, which would moreover be the just price, in order to carry out exchange.

[14] In this line, we have to mention Schumpeter ([1954] 2006, 89) and to a lesser extent Langholm (1992, 228–233) and Sivéry (2004, 703). About the classical debate on Thomasian just price, see Dempsey (1935); Worland (1977); Lapidus (1986, 18); Lapidus (1992, 29–30); Lapidus (1994, 435); Franks (2009, 85–92); Santori (2020, 281–282).

Secondly, several clues scattered throughout *De emptione* confirm that the current literature is right to distance itself from the traditional terms of the debate. The just price may cover the costs of production and manifest itself on the market, but it is first and foremost a price of justice. And it is only the effective manifestation of justice, which pre-exists it. Indeed, the reflection on the just price is part of the Thomasian treatment of the virtue of justice itself. Aquinas does not base his analysis on a price of charity, a price of efficiency, or some other qualifier, but on a "just" price, thus a price that conforms to the virtue of justice. This is reflected in *De emptione* in two ways: first, by the notion of approximation, introduced by "*aestimatio*", since an approximation is made in relation to a reference value, which remains hidden and which one seeks to manifest, with a margin of error; and second, by Aquinas's use of the expression "according to [*secundum*] the common market". But *secundum* introduces a notion of conformity with a reference without establishing an identity (Quicherat 1893, 1013; Ernout and Meillet 2001, 608). The singular just price is therefore not the just price on the market. Three levels thus emerge: the just price is a price of justice, which manifests itself when it is estimated on the market and which manifests itself in the singular exchange, in accordance with this estimate on the market, but without being identical to it.

A second risk then appears, following the first one, which concerns the estimation as an approximation. Aquinas refers both to the price and to the value: so there is at least a conceptual gap between value and price, but this distinction is rarely made in the literature, which often equates the two notions (typically De Roover 1958, 422 and De Roover 1971, 52 and 56–61), with the notable exception of Bartell (1962) and Lapidus's reservations (1986, 17–28 and 1994, 440). Yet this distinction is necessary. Indeed, the term "*pretium*" (price) appears only in *De emptione*, I. Usury occurs when "the good is sold for more than the just price because of the expectation [*ultra quantitatem iusti pretii propter expectationem*]" and the contract "is priced for the time of expectation [*cum expectatio temporis sub pretio cadat*]". The value only appears in *De emptione*, II and III, at the time of the sale transaction. There is usury when the cloths are sold for "more than they are worth [*plus quam valeant*]". The use of two different terms, the noun "price" and the verb "to be worth", in two distinct places, though unified by the discussion of usury, shows that one cannot be equated with the other.

Whereas it is accepted that price can vary, the stability of value is not clearly established in Aquinas's works. Indeed, Aquinas does not speak of "price" in the common market, but of what a good is "worth" in that market. The value is the pivot of reference, but this does not prejudge its fixed character. The text of *De emptione* can be interpreted in three ways. First, one could consider that value varies with the price of the good in the market. However, Aquinas is careful not to identify value and price; it seems rather that he is positing a conformity between an actual just price and a value. A second assumption would be that the value could incorporate the cost of the delay in payment. However, extrinsic titles, which in Roman law ensure the remuneration of the loan by means of ancillary contracts, are external to the property; it could then be said that the non-usurious price transcribes, beyond the value of the good, an exchange relation that integrates an acceptable surplus. Finally, value can be understood as stable and "*secundum se*". Nothing explicitly states that value varies in the market, and Aquinas refers value to the good exchanged and not to the agents; however, he does not explicitly formulate value as "*secundum se*", and it does not seem possible to rule definitively on whether value fluctuates or what components it incorporates. The only conclusion that can be drawn is the formal distinction between value and price.

The link between price and value is ensured by the situation of usury, if the sale is not made at the just price (*De emptione*, I) and if one sells the goods for more than they are worth (*De emptione*, II and III). Aquinas's use of the notion of value shows that it is broader than the notion of price, even though the just price is consistent with value and appears as its transaction in exchange. The conceptual gap between value and price introduces a risk of error in the transcription of the value into the actual price in the course of the exchange.

The highlighting of this discrepancy as early as *De emptione* makes it possible to identify something in the *Summa theologiae* that has never been emphasised, and which remains an object of confusion. Thus, when Aquinas states that it is "the quantity [*quantitas*] of things which come to the use of men which is measured according to the price given [*mensuratur secundum pretium datum*]" (*S. T.*, IIa IIae, q. 77, a.1, resp.), utility and need refer here to price, although no mention is made of value, contrary to the French translation by Spicq in 1935 which translates *quantitas* as "quantity or value". The value then appears only to represent the link between the thing and the price, thus affirming the need for conformity but not a formal identity: "if the price exceeds the quantity of the value of the thing [*quantitatem valoris rei*], or conversely if the thing exceeds the price [*res excedat pretium*]", and then in the concluding sentence: "therefore to sell more [*carius*] or buy less [*vilius*] than it is worth is in itself unjust and illicit" (*S. T.*, IIa IIae, q. 77, a.1, resp.). Moreover, the value seems to be distinguished immediately afterwards from the effective just price, which takes account of utility and prejudice: "The just price must be established not only in regard to the thing sold [*respiciatur ad rem quae venditur*], but in proportion to the prejudice suffered by the seller" (*S. T.*, IIa IIae, q. 77, a.1, resp.), whereas Spicq (1935) introduces "value" for *respiciatur*, where the Latin does not mention it. Thus, the just price integrates and transcribes utility, need and prejudice, rather than the value from which it derives (Bartell 1962, 333).

In addition, Aquinas does not define value univocally but unites two meanings in the same sentence: the intrinsic value, *secundum se*, of the thing, and the value for the possessor: "One may licitly sell something beyond its intrinsic value [*plus quam valeat secundum se*], although it is not sold for more than it is worth to the possessor [*plus quam valeat habenti*]" (*S. T.*, IIa IIae, q. 77, a.1, resp.). So, value remains a polysemic noun and what it refers to remains unclear. In *S. T.*, IIa IIae, q. 77, a.1, obj. 3, value appears more as a value *secundum se* which does not integrate utility and need, as compensation for a benefit (*beneficium*) sometimes exceeds the value of the thing (*excedit valorem rei datae*) if the need for the thing is great. This leads to a dissociation between price and value: it is permissible to exchange at a price higher than what the thing is worth (*pro majori pretio quam valeat*), and this is not resolved in the answer. *S. T.*, IIa IIae, q. 77, a. 3, ad 4 and *S. T.*, IIa IIae, q. 77, a. 4, ad 2 also show multiple understandings of value, its content, its variation and its relationship to price (Januard 2022d). A reading of *De emptione* thus leads to attention being paid to a conceptual distinction that is present in the *Summa theologiae* but ignored by its readers, and to the risks it entails.

De emptione thus provides new elements for understanding Thomasian risk:

1. There is a universalisation of usurious risk to all agents. This universalisation occurs in two ways:
   (a) On the one hand, it is a sale of goods and not a monetary loan. The agents potentially concerned by the usury situation are sellers and buyers and no longer only lenders and borrowers as in *In III Sent.*, d. 37, a. 6.

(b) On the other hand, the situation of requesting a discount for early payment raises the paradoxical possibility that the borrower will cause the lender to incur a price prejudice, since the transaction would then be below the just price due to time.

2. The notion of estimation as an approximation creates a risk in the determination of the just price, which can be misunderstood or miscalculated.
3. The conceptual gap between value and price leads to a risk of non-conformity of the actual price of the exchange with the value of the exchanged good when the value is translated into a price.
4. A certain indeterminacy in the notion of value and in the possible fluctuation of this value increases the risk of error in the transcription of value into price.
5. Aquinas's expression of the role of the market presents an ambiguity that has fuelled the main debate among commentators on Aquinas's economic thought for the past hundred years. There is thus a risk of attributing to the market the ability to determine and form the right price, and hence of considering any market price as a right price.

This leads to new risks:[15]

RUde1: A risk that buyers and sellers in commercial operations may be involved in an usurious transaction.

RUde2: A risk that the buyer/borrower becomes a usurer if he asks for a discount that puts the price below the just price.

RTde3: A risk in the determination of the just price due to the fact that estimation is understood as an approximation.

RUde4: A risk of non-conformity of the actual price of the exchange with the value of the exchanged good when the value is translated into a price.

RUde5: An analysis of risk on value due to a certain indeterminacy in this notion.

RUde6: An analysis of risk on the role of the market as "just price taker" or "just price maker".

De emptione thus complements the *Commentary on the Sentences* in two ways. On the one hand, this text confirms the unified vision of economic activity through the treatment of a transaction that is both commerce and

[15] Risks on usury in *De emptione*, numbered "RUde".

usury, and by making price the criterion of justice. On the other hand, *De emptione* proceeds to universalise the usurious risk, which in the *Commentary on the Sentences* was still unidirectional from the lender to the borrower, and highlights new risks, which sound like an implementation of the risk analysis of the activity underlined in *In III Sent.*, d. 37, a. 6, since they are risks concerning the notions of value and market. *De emptione* also renews our reading of the *Summa theologiae* by drawing attention to this gap between value and price, which is often ignored, and suggests, through the unification it pursues after the *Commentary on the Sentences*, that we read q. 77 on commercial fraud and q. 78 in a common perspective (*S. T.*, IIa IIae, q. 77–78), as the prologue to these two questions indeed invites us to do.

Risks to the Activity of Merchants

Thomas Aquinas addresses the activity of merchants twice in his early works: first in the *Commentary on the Sentences*, where he deals briefly with the general conditions of the professional merchant's activity in a subquestion of Book IV, after having studied the question of usury in an article of Book III, and then in *De emptione*, where the treatment of forward sales leads him to mention, again briefly, a more general point that concerns all sales, namely the distinction between the costs that the seller may or may not pass on in the selling price. Thus, the early works do not offer a treatise on the justice of commercial exchange as the *Summa theologiae* will. However, these two texts highlight certain risks which have not been stressed before, and which do not afterwards appear explicitly in Aquinas's works, but which constitute implicit foundations for later Thomasian developments. These texts establish the two dimensions of commercial justice: a qualitative dimension (who, when and how we exchange) and a quantitative dimension (at what price we exchange). Each of these two dimensions involves a risk that the conditions for a just exchange should not be fulfilled. Firstly, the *Commentary on the Sentences* sets out the general framework for the activity of merchants. It does not pronounce on the morality of the purpose of trade, but on the morality of its means. Where his predecessors, a century earlier, did not consider that merchants could practice their trade without sin, Aquinas is more open. If the activity can be just or unjust, justice is possible without being certain, which gives rise to a risk of injustice in the exchange. Secondly, *De emptione*, for its part, highlights the risk incurred by merchants because of the lack of certainty that the merchant has, when making the expenditure, about the price and quantity of the sale. In addition, the notion of prudence allows Aquinas to identify expenses that are licitly incurred, which the merchant can pass on in the price, and those that are not. The buyer thus runs the risk that illicit expenses will nevertheless be included in the price.

The General Framework of the Merchants' Activity: Qualitative and Quantitative Risks

Thomas Aquinas focuses on trade in the third sub-question of an article on contentious activities, *In IV Sent.*, d. 16, q. 4, a. 2, qc. 3, in the context of a *distinctio* devoted to penance. This sub-question is entitled: "It seems that military or trade practice does not prevent penance". The treatment of trade is therefore moral and sacramental. Not only is this text very brief (a scant 304 words), but trade is not even addressed for its own sake. Indeed, Aquinas here is treating of three potentially sinful occupations, that of the merchant, of the soldier and of the publican, within a question on impediments to true penance and, within that question, an article on gambling.

Let us note that the question here concerns trade in the sense of a professional activity for gain, the activity of negotiation, or *exercitium negotiationis*. It involves the same type of merchant that would be mentioned a few years later in *De emptione*, and a few years later still in *De regno* where Aquinas addresses the issue of supply and the social and cultural impact of the arrival of foreign merchants. But Aquinas does not here address commerce in the sense of exchanges for the necessities of life, according to the distinction that he will make in *S. T.*, IIa IIae, q. 77, a. 4, resp. (Franks 2009, 100–101; Dellemotte 2017, 36–39; Koehler 2020, 362).

It is not until the later works that Aquinas would deal with commercial trading in general, regardless of the social status of the merchant. This is the case in the *Summa theologiae*, where only the fourth and last article of the question on commercial fraud deals explicitly with the professional merchants who act "for gain [*propter lucrum*]" (*S. T.*, IIa IIae, q. 77, a. 4, resp.), whereas the general case simply considers that the purchase and sale takes place "for the common utility of both parties [*pro communi utilitate utriusque*]" (*S. T.*, IIa IIae, q. 77, a. 1, resp.), without necessarily involving a professional activity with a view to enrichment. However, the attention paid to merchants in his youthful works provides the general framework for analysing exchange.

As Aquinas deals conjointly with two activities, namely that of the soldier (*exercitium militiae*) and that of the merchant (*exercitium negotiationis*), echoing Peter Lombard (*IV Sent.*, d. 16, c. 3), this parallelism makes it possible to highlight by contrast the specific character of Aquinas's treatment of the activity of the merchant.

A preliminary risk appears on reading Aquinas: the risk of analysis on his part. An error of understanding could arise from Aquinas's own subjectivity, as the son and brother of knights (Weisheipl [1974] 1993, 16–19; Torrell 2015, 20–25; Januard 2022c) and even a *chevalier manqué* (Synan 1988, 437), and in particular his view of merchants, a new social class evincing a rapid and suspicious enrichment. For Aquinas, the knight who falls into disgrace drops down into the ranks of peasants and merchants (*S. T.*, Ia IIae, q. 91, a. 6, resp.; Synan 1988, 419–420). However, since Aquinas took a more open position on the activity of merchants than his predecessors, even though nothing from his family's point of view seemed to dispose him to do so, this risk of subjective bias can be considered low, but formally, it still remains.

The first risk for merchants is then the risk on the licitness of their activity. For the Bible indeed stresses that it is "difficult for traders to avoid sin" (Ecclesiasticus 26:28). Gregory VII considered in 1078 that the soldier and the merchant "cannot practice without sin [*sine peccato exerceri non possint*]" (Gregory VII, *Concilium Romanum* V, col. 801, B-C), and Gratian (*Decretum*, II, causa 33, q. 3 De poenitentia, d. 5, c. 6) and Peter Lombard (*IV Sent.*, d. 16, c. 3) took up this text respectively around 1140 and 1150, in line with the Fathers of the Church (on the progressive permission of trade, see O'Brien [1920] 2001). Albert the Great takes a more open position on the biblical text, which simply indicates the difficulty, not the impossibility, of trading without sinning (Albert, *In IV Sent.*, d. 16, a. 46, s. c.), and which allows him to concentrate on the conditions of the justice of trading (*In IV Sent.*, d. 16, a. 46, resp. ad q. 1). Aquinas follows Albert: he evokes Gregory's position in the *sed contra*, the key to the article, but he does not return to it in his *respondeo*, the core of the article, where he gives his position, which consists, as for Albert, in establishing the licit conditions of commercial activity. Fifteen years later, in the *Summa theologiae*, we find the same position of the need to regulate mercantile activity, without, however, prohibiting it or considering merchants to be necessarily in a state of sin: "fraud and deceit are usually practised in matters of buying and selling [...] for this reason, there is in the law a special prohibitive precept with regard to fraud committed in buying and selling" (*S. T.*, IIa IIae, q. 56, a. 2, ad 2). The variations in interpretation of the biblical verse on the sinfulness of merchants throughout history create a risk of the licitness of merchants depending on the consideration of their sinful state and the prohibition of their activity.

We see, then, that the first category of risk, although not explicitly formulated, is that of the risk of analysis, since Gratian and Peter Lombard, on the one hand, and Albert and Aquinas, on the other hand, make a different reading of the same biblical verse governing trade with regard to what they perceive to be the reality of mercantile activity. Furthermore, in a society in which social belonging is of decisive importance, the observer's position is partly conditioned by his or her own personal relationship with the new social category of merchants.

Having been able to establish, from the *sed contra*, an analysis risk relating to the understanding of the activity and its morality, we see that the rest of the sub-question implements a derivative form of this analysis risk. It is no longer a risk of error, but a risk of other concerns: this is the case with procurement. Aquinas does not make a statement in the sub-question about the purpose of trade. He merely stresses the necessity of supply at the beginning of his text, in *objectio* 1, but does not return to it in the *respondeo*. This necessity thus seems to be taken for granted (Baldwin 1959, 64–65; Dupuy 1992, 38–41), but is not particularly emphasised. It is developed a few years later in *De regno*, II, 7 (II, 3), where it ambivalently justifies merchant activity, but even more so encourages local production in the face of the social mischief produced by the arrival in the city of merchants, understood here as professionals from afar. In the end, Aquinas's relationship to supply remains ambiguous (Januard 2024b, 522–531). In *Ethicorum*, V, 9, he differs from his authorities (Langholm 1984, 32) by not noting, contrary to Aristotle (*Nicomachean Ethics*, V, 5, 1133a) and especially to Albert the Great in his two commentaries on Aristotle's *Ethics* (*Ethicorum*, written in 1250–1252, ed. Cologne, V, VII, 403–404 and V, IX, 413 (see Kübel 1968–1972, VI); and *Ethicorum*, written after 1260, ed. Borgnet, V, II, 9), that the cessation of exchange resulting from the absence of a just price (Hollander 1965, 619–621) will affect all crafts and lead to the fall of the city (Hamouda and Price 1997, 195). The *Summa theologiae* unites utility and the good purpose of trade by considering the possibility of a good purpose of professional activity for gain (*propter lucrum*), if it is done for a moderate gain (*lucrum moderatum*) and if this gain is ordered (*ordinari*) to a necessary and honest end (*aliquam finem necessarium, vel estiam honestium*). The three good ends are to feed one's household, to help the needy and to supply the country (*S. T.*, IIa IIae, q. 77, a. 4, resp.).

We can see that what emerges allusively from the *Commentary on the Sentences* is confirmed later on: Aquinas knows that trade is necessary for supply, which is itself necessary for the city, but his concern lies elsewhere. In this way, supply acts as a sort of inclusive framework: a quick but clear mention at the beginning of the first text on trade (*In IV Sent.*, d. 16, q. 4, a. 2, qc. 3, obj. 1) and at the end of the last one (*S. T.*, IIa IIae, q. 77, a. 4, resp.), and an ambiguous evocation, then an absence, in the intermediate writings. More than the supply, what matters for Aquinas is the justice of the exchange, to the point that the requirement that the merchant's gain be moderate (*lucrum moderatum*) increases the risk of scarcity, since if the gain is too small, or if it is not a net profit but a gain on which the merchant has charges to pay, moderation can constitute a disincentive. Aquinas does not remark on this. Moreover, in the later works, the necessity of supply seems to fade: it is absent from the *Commentary on Nicomachean Ethics*, and in the *Summa theologiae* supply constitutes a good end that legitimises trade, but Aquinas does not elaborate on its necessity, limiting himself to mentioning the adjective "*necessarium*".

The primacy of the concern for the justice of exchange over that of supply thus constitutes a new variant of the analysis risk. This risk is all the more worth emphasising as it concerns, beyond merchants, the whole population, which may be confronted with a shortage.

Having noted this risk pertaining to Aquinas's own interests, however, it is worth noting how Aquinas limits the risk of agents in the *Commentary on the Sentences*. Supply is a necessity, but not yet an end, as in the *Summa theologiae*. Aquinas does not pronounce on the final end because, in the absence of an objective that is structured around the moderation of gain and the three good ends (*S. T.*, IIa IIae, q. 77, a. 4 resp.), the only final end is subjective, according to the agent's intention. But this intention remains hidden. The risk on the final end of trade therefore only disappears in the *Summa theologiae*. However, Aquinas minimises this risk by bypassing the question of finality by focusing on the licitness of the means, that is, on the conditions for the practice of trade.

Aquinas therefore confines himself in the *respondeo* to formulating the conditions for the licit practice of trade, taking up the triptych *persona* (person), *tempus* (time) and *modus* (mode) of Albert the Great (Albert, *In IV Sent.*, d. 16, a. 46, resp. ad q. 1), although he does not formally mention this triptych.

Persona. Firstly, for Aquinas, the merchant "must not be in a condition which prevents him from doing so by his office, so that trading is not permitted [*non licet negotiari*] to clerics and monks, although they may sell their own goods" (*In IV Sent.*, d. 16, q. 4, a. 2, qc. 3, resp.). This first criterion does not present a significant risk because there is little risk of error on the person. It should be noted here that clerics and monks are forbidden to trade professionally for gain, in the sense of the *negotio* referred to in the *Commentary on the Sentences*, but not to buy and sell "for the necessity of life [*ad necessitate vitae*]" (*S. T.*, IIa IIae, q. 77, a. 4, ad 3), as Aquinas makes clear in the *Summa theologiae*.

Tempus. Trade is also prohibited on certain days of the year: "trade must be done at the appropriate time [*tempore debito*], and not on feast days, and such a function must not be practiced at a time which may lead to feasting" (*In IV Sent.*, d. 16, q. 4, a. 2, qc. 3, resp.). Knowing that non-working days represent, depending on the guild, between a quarter and more than a third of the days of the year (Ellul 2013, 229; Verdon 2016, 13–19), the restriction of *tempus* is real and binding. This is therefore a constraint, but not a risk, since the timetable is known, with few possible errors. These first two criteria are qualitative and are therefore risk-free for both the merchant and the customer.

Modus. Finally comes the condition of *modus*: "the mode due, as without committing fraud and according to a licit contract [*et modus debitus, ut sine fraude fiat, et secundum licitum contractum*]" (*In IV Sent.*, d. 16, q. 4, a. 2, qc. 3, resp.). This third criterion, the *modus*, is important because positive law of contracts has a decisive role in the protection of co-contractors for the mediaeval scholastics (Ege 2014, 408–409; Santori 2021, 21). The *modus* is both qualitative and quantitative. Indeed, each of its two terms, "without fraud" and "according to a licit contract", has a quantitative and a qualitative dimension. Fraud may relate to the price, but also to the property or the framework of the exchange, just as the contract may relate to the determination of the price but also governs the qualitative modalities of the exchange. The risk of injustice in the exchange may therefore relate to the qualitative criteria of justice: while we have seen that the risk on the person and on the day is low, risk may concern the existence of fraud (which may occur on the nature, the quantity or quality of the object exchanged, as Aquinas details in *S. T.*, IIa IIae, q. 77, a.2, resp.), of fraud on the actual non-financial conditions of the exchange, or of mistakes in the contractual formalisation of the exchange, namely that the contract is not licitly made or that the exchange is not made in accordance with the contract. This risk can also be a quantitative risk on the price, if the just price is not applied due to fraud, if the contractual price is not just, or if the just contractual price is not applied.

Aquinas's later writings do not formally take up the triptych *persona, tempus, modus*. However, it can be seen that it constitutes the inaugural framework, which remains in place at least tacitly thereafter. The prohibition of professional trade for gain (*ordinata ad lucrum terrenum*) is maintained for clerics (there is no longer any mention of monks) in *S. T.*, IIa IIae, q. 77, a. 4, ad 3. Holidays are no longer explicitly mentioned. *Modus* is still addressed through fraud and contract (*S. T.*, IIa IIae, q. 77, a. 1, resp.), or through a variation in terms of virtue and law (*II Quodl.*, q. 5, a. 2). We thus observe on the one hand that the inaugural framework, based on qualitative and quantitative criteria of justice, and thus qualitative and quantitative risks of injustice, remains, and on the other hand that it is the *modus* that will be the object of deeper reflection. Indeed, while the clerical identity of the person or the holiday character of the day is known to all, the notions of fraud and respect for the licitly made contract need to be clarified. The additions made in the *Summa theologiae* thus provide elements to reduce the risk that was highlighted in the *Commentary on the Sentences*.

Aquinas does not define fraud. The *Commentary on the Sentences* therefore carries a risk for agents in terms of the qualitative and quantitative interpretation of fraud. However, this concept takes up the two traditional principles of *turpe lucrum* (dishonest gain) and *laesio enormis* (significant prejudice), although without being sufficiently precise. *Turpe lucrum* (Langholm 2003, 36) can be found, for example, in Gratian's *Decree* (*Decretum*, II, causa 14, q. 4, c. 9), where it describes a gain of more than double (the sale price is twice the purchase price) with speculative intent. *Laesio enormis*, a concept originally used to protect the heir to land, has been expanded to protect the seller from a transfer of property at less than half the original price (Baldwin 1959, 23–24; De Roover 1971, 53; Lapidus 1992, 41; Lupton 2015, 520–521; Chaplygina and Lapidus 2016, 21). The general rule is thus that of *duplus*, with the sale having to be made at between half and twice the purchase price. Whereas Aquinas takes up this rule precisely in the *Summa theologiae* (*S. T.*, IIa IIae, q. 77,

a. 1, ad 1), the *Commentary on the Sentences*, by sticking to a general expression of absence of fraud, introduces a risk concerning the indeterminacy of the level from which the price becomes unjust.

Finally, in *In IV Sent.*, d. 16, q. 4, a. 2, qc. 3, only the merchant is obliged to refrain from fraud, which implies a maximum price limit. Nothing is said about any protection against downward pressure on the price. Thus, the seller runs a remuneration risk, since his maximum gain is limited while his maximum loss is not. This limit to the possible price rise will be affirmed even more strongly in the *Summa theologiae* with the notion of "moderate gain [*lucrum moderatum*]" in *S. T.*, IIa IIae, q. 77, a. 4, resp. Yet this leads to a risk for the whole society, for the limitation of gain is not precisely determined. It is not known whether it is a net or gross gain, a limited profit or a revenue on which the merchant must pay charges. In accounting terms, while the term "gain" suggests that it is not just a turnover, it does not specify to which intermediate operating total it refers. If it is not the net profit but an intermediate balance such as a gross operating surplus, the outstanding expenses may lead to a negative net result. The requirement of moderate gain may then ultimately result in a loss that would dissuade merchants from practising their profession, and thus from supplying the country. However, the nature of the merchant's gain both confirms the moderation of this gain and limits the hypothesis of a risk of loss and a halt in supply. Indeed, the merchant receives a "*quasi stipendium laboris* [as a stipend for labour]" (Januard 2022c, 85–91), a compensation for his social utility. Whereas *praemium*, used for the merchant-craftsman (*S. T.*, IIa IIae, q. 77, a. 4, ad 1), evokes a price and a proportionality between work and income—*praemium* is thought of as "the price of work [*pretium laboris*]" (*De veritate*, q. 26, a. 6, obj. 10)—like the wage (Rocha 1933, 10–20, Lapidus 1994, 441; Rajapakse 2010, 207–210; Noell 1998, 476), and must be just, like the price (Hirschfeld 2018, 188–189), *stipendium* refers to the stipend of the soldier (*In IV Sent.*, d. 25, q. 3, a. 2, qc. 1, obj. 4), the priest (*S. T.*, IIa IIae, q. 100, a. 2, resp.), or, in the exact form "*quasi stipendium laboris*", to the witnesses (*S. T.*, IIa IIae, q. 71, a. 4, ad 3) as social compensation for their work, and to the tribute due to the king (*ad Romanos*, c. 13, l. 1, 1041).

A series of risks appear, therefore, in Aquinas's first text on the activity of merchants. First, there is a plurality of analytical risks:[16]

[16] Risks on trade in the *Commentary on the Sentences*, *In IV Sent.*, d. 16, q. 4, a. 2, qc. 3, numbered "RTcs".

RTcs1: A risk in the understanding of commercial activity, as shown by the difference in position between Gratian and Peter Lombard on the one hand and Albert and Aquinas on the other hand.

RTcs2: A risk of subjective bias in the understanding of this activity, due to Aquinas's aristocratic background relative to the suspicious new social category of merchants.

RTcs3: A risk of scarcity because of Aquinas's emphasis on the justice of exchange rather than supply, although this need is perceived.

RTcs4: A risk on the just price and on the fair conditions of the exchange because of the general and relatively allusive nature of the notion of fraud.

RTcs5: A risk of shortage due to a halt in trade if the conditions imposed on merchants are disincentives through the notion of fraud.

From these analysis, risks arise a risk of scarcity for the city, and two risks for merchants:

RTcs6: A risk to the licitness of the activity.

RTcs7: A risk of remuneration, since the price has an upper bound by the notion of fraud but nothing protects the seller from an unfairly low price demanded by the buyer.

We can add three commercial risks, which are risks coming from outside the exchange:

RTcs8: A risk that, even without fraud, the current price is not advantageous or that qualitative conditions are too restrictive.

RTcs9: A risk that, even without fraud, the current price or qualitative conditions are unfair by mistake.

RTcs10: A risk that the contract contains damaging errors.

We can also add two strategic risks, one for the merchant and one for the customer, due to the hidden motivation of the co-contractor:

RTcs11: A risk of fraud by the merchant.

RTcs12: A risk of the customer misrepresenting the merchant as a fraudster.

The clarifications provided by subsequent works would, on the one hand, reduce the risks of analysis due to the imprecision of the notion of fraud and, on the other hand, confirm the conditional licitness of the commercial activity and thus reduce the risk that concerns the existence of the activity itself. Conversely, the ambiguity of the place occupied by the need for supply will be confirmed, and this risk, which concerns the entire population, would therefore be reinforced. The commercial risk remains, since the price varies according to place and time (*S. T.*, IIa IIae, q. 77, a. 4, ad.

2), but the formal notion of contract fades away, reducing the risk of contractual error. The explicit use of the notion of just price will reduce the strategic risk by providing an objective and visible criterion of the justice of the exchange. Alongside these developments, the structural analysis of the justice of exchange as qualitative and quantitative, founded in the *Commentary on the Sentences*, remains in the later works. The risk weighing on commercial activity is thus confirmed in its two dimensions, qualitative and quantitative.

Risks on Licit and Illicit Spending by Merchants

Thomas Aquinas continues his analysis of the activity of merchants in *De emptione*. Whereas the first two sections of this short letter deal specifically with forward sales, the third section widens the scope to the entire market activity in order to establish what is licitly or nominally acceptable for the merchant to include in the selling price. As we have seen, the literature has traditionally retained two Thomasian approaches to the just price: the approach by production costs, as supported by Tawney ([1926] 1948, 41) from the expression of *Ethicorum*, V, 9, "in labour and expenses [*in labore et expensis*]"; and the approach by the market, developed in particular by De Roover (1971, 59), from the expression of *De emptione*, II, "according to the market [*secundum communem forum*]". In *De emptione*, III, we find a complement to the production cost approach, since the account here is not, as in *Ethicorum*, V, 9, about the costs of the producer-seller, but about the costs of the professional merchant who buys to resell. It is therefore, in a way, the merchant's production costs to produce a service, which is essentially a service of transport and supply. In *De emptione*, the two approaches to the Thomasian just price (production-based and market-based approaches) are thus brought together, since it is a price that conforms to the price found on the market when the latter is just and that integrates licit costs, although commentators have often wanted to oppose these two approaches, with the exception of attempts to combine them, with a market price that gravitates around the costs of production (Hollander 1965).

Some expenses, such as transport, can be included in the sale price; others, such as loan expenses and expenses incurred through imprudence, cannot (Januard 2022b; Januard 2024a, 430–432). All of these expenses are risky, as their recovery is not certain since the quantity demanded and the price that will be charged on the market at the time and place of sale are not known and may vary. They can therefore be treated as a price risk, that is, a risk that the expenses will not be covered by the selling price. In addition, there is a risk for the merchant that his expenses are illegal and that he cannot include them in the price, and a risk for the buyer that the merchant should have included these expenses in the price anyway and that the sale is thus made above the just price.

Transport is presented in *De emptione*, III as the ultimate licit expenditure, because it constitutes the merchant's own proper and professional activity (Baldwin 1959, 65, 77; Hollander 1965, 627, 630, 632). Although transport is merely given as an example and is not the only licitly incurred expense, it is the only one named: "It is, on the other hand, permissible [*et licet*] for them to recover licitly [*possint licite recuperare*] by their sale other expenses [*expensas alias*] licitly incurred [*licite factas*], for example, for the transport of the cloths [*puta in portatione pannorum*]" (*De emptione*, III). Transport is notoriously risky (Spicq 1935, 349–354; Franks 2009, 82; Dellemotte 2017, 38) and costly (Sturn 2017, 650), even though during the Middle Ages, the development of carriage transport across the Alps and the securing of sea and land routes brought down this cost (Persson 2014, 253).

Fifteen years later, the *Summa theologiae* would make a twofold change in its treatment of the risk of transport. First, the conception of transport has evolved. In *De emptione*, although it concerns a long-distance journey, from Italy to the Lagny fair near Paris, this is a case of overland transport, no doubt managed individually, which essentially constitutes an operation of physical displacement as rendered by the expression "*in portatione pannorum*", literally the expenses "in the carrying of cloth". Ten years later, Aquinas no longer refers to an expense but to "a danger [or risk, *periculum*] to which someone is exposed [*exponit*] by transferring from one place to another [*transferendo rem de loco ad locum*]" (*S. T.*, IIa IIae, q. 77, a. 4, ad 2). The new emphasis is more on the distance and the movement of travel than on the physical work of transport. It is a more geographical and abstract approach to transport that insists on the change of place. Transport acquires a new status and becomes an economic activity in its own right, carried out by professionals whose task is to transport a good from one place to another, under the threat, expressed by the noun *periculum*, of theft or shipwreck (Januard 2024a, 432–436). Transport is one of the two reasons, along with the improvement of the good by the craftsman, which justifies selling a good for more than it was purchased (*S. T.*, IIa IIae, q. 77, a. 4, ad 2).

Aquinas then mentions illicit expenditures, the first of which is the expenditure made by merchants who borrow money at interest: "But they cannot recover the usury they pay" (*De emptione*, III). This is not given as an example but rather as a statement of the generic form of illicit expenditure to which the following merely refers. It is an "unjust payment" by which merchants commit the sin of usury by giving usurers the opportunity to sin. Aquinas is very severe regarding merchants who borrow but do not do so out of real necessity: "the necessity that is put forward [*ponitur*] to live more honourably and to do more business [*maiores mercationes faciant*] is not sufficient to exempt them from this sin" (*De emptione*, III). He thus remarks on the fact that such borrowing does indeed happen, and that the operation is for personal benefit and not for the common good, and highlights the subjective nature of the justification by the expression "*cum necessitas quae ponitur* [the necessity that is put forward]" (*De emptione*, III).

Thus, there are three respects in which Aquinas distances himself from the idea of a loan for production or trade:

1. The development of the activity is secondary to the morality of the operation.
2. The need for this development is referred to a subjective and self-interested expression on the part of the merchants, without any reference to the social necessity of trade.
3. The usefulness of borrowing to ensure this development is referred to this same subjectivity, without being established in an objective manner.

It must be added that even in the case of a licitly incurred expense such as transport, the licitness of the expense does not entail that the method of financing is also licit. Thus, whereas in *De emptione* Aquinas only addresses the licit nature of the expense of transport, 15 years later in the *Summa theologiae*, he specifies the licit conditions of its financing, through the acquisition of a share in a *societas* (a partnership in which the investor puts the money and the merchant proceeds with the trade) and not through an interest-bearing loan (see Spicq 1935, 349–351; du Passage 1946, col. 2361; Sivéry 2004, 698; Ege 2014, 403; Chaplygina and Lapidus 2016, 37; Chaplygina and Lapidus 2022). In the *societas* model, the investor remains the owner of the money invested and therefore bears the risk of loss, which legitimises the possibility of receiving a gain, that is, a share of the profits, which is not the case in a loan, which must be made without interest:

> [The lender] must not demand [*exigere*] more than he has given [*mutavit*]. But he who entrusts [*commitit*] his money to a merchant or craftsman by the mode of a kind of partnership [*per modum societatis cujusdam*] does not transfer in it the ownership of his money, which remains his, so that at his own risk [cum *periculo ipsius*] the merchant trades or the craftsman fabricates. Thus, he may licitly seek [*expetere*] a share of the profits [*partem lucri*] derived therefrom, as something belonging to him. (*S. T.*, IIa IIae, q. 78, a. 2, ad 5)

Borrowing is therefore not seen by Aquinas as a legitimate means of developing economic activity. However, the proposal of a licit alternative, the *societas*, made immediately after his remarks on the impossibility of an interest-bearing loan, testifies to Aquinas's openness to production and trade and to the need for its financing (Monsalve 2014b, 227–228).[17]

It should be noted, however, that a decisive step has been taken, since Aquinas thereby departs from the tradition of the Fathers, as represented, a few years before him, by William of Auxerre, who sees in the loan the systematic oppression of the poor, who are subject to constraint, and instead adopts a social approach to usury: "Usury is directly against charity [*dare ad usuram directe est contra caritatem*]" (William of Auxerre, *Summa aurea*, III, XLVIII, c. 1, q. 1, l. 5). While remaining prohibited, the interest-bearing loan is thought of here within the professional framework of market activity. It is a question of licitly financing a licit activity—namely, in both *De emptione* and *Summa theologiae*, transport—which respects the link between property, risk and gain.

[17] It was not until the end of the thirteenth century, and the *Treatise on Contracts* (c. 1293) by the Franciscan Peter John Olivi, that we see the clear appearance of the idea of capital invested in risky operations that was not a gratuitous *mutuum* and did not fall under the prohibition of usury, although it did not fall within the model of the *societas*. However, surplus is still only rooted in risk (Kirshner and Lo Prete 1984; Ceccarelli 1999; Piron 2012; Kaye [1998] 2004; Toivanen 2016). The Franciscan Gerard or Gerald Odonis (or Guiral Ot) wrote his *Liber de contractibus et restitutionibus et de sententia excommunicationis* in 1315–1317. This treatise takes up Olivi's theses, but it adopts a new analytical framework for thinking about interest lending and thus foreshadows the developments of the modern era. The prejudice caused by the loan makes interest legitimate and, following the bull *Exiit qui seminat* (1279), Odonis separates ownership from use. Odonis no longer follows the complex discussions around the different extrinsic titles, but directly considers the "sale of time", legitimised by the social utility of merchants (the justification by the common good was already found in Olivi) and the need for a payment term for long-distance trade. Henceforth, it is no longer the risk that justifies the surplus but the time (Piron 1997; Ceccarelli and Piron 2009).

We can conclude that Aquinas's thought on licit and illicit expenditure progressively takes into account more complex situations. In *De emptione*, Aquinas presents a licit expenditure, the cost of transport, and an illicit one, the cost of a loan. Ten years later in the *Summa theologiae*, Aquinas unifies these cases by combining these two expenses: it is illicit to finance transport by an interest-bearing loan, that is, to fund a licit expenditure by an illicit one.

Having addressed the case of interest-bearing loans, Aquinas then evokes other illicit expenses, namely imprudent expenditure: "In a similar way it is evident [*patet enim similia*] that one cannot recover the expenses incurred without precauton [*incaute*] and unwisely [*imprudenter*]" (*De emptione*, III). The juxtaposition of borrowing and imprudent expenditure can be understood either as an enumeration or as an expansion, where borrowing would represent the imprudent expenditure par excellence. The doubt cast on the motives of the merchants rather suggests that borrowing is the imprudence par excellence, the profit motive leading to an expenditure made without precaution or unwisely.

Thomasian prudence is a virtue, a good *habitus* (*In III Sent.*, d. 33, q. 2; *S. T.*, IIa IIae, q. 47 to 56; see Daubercies 1990). As a cardinal virtue, it is linked to justice (Baldwin 1959, 59; Bartell 1962, 338; Langholm 2003, 86; Hirschfeld 2018, 106; Rajapakse 2010, 250). We can thus see that imprudence would lead to injustice, namely an unjust price, if imprudent expenditures were passed on in the price. As a virtue, prudence cannot therefore at first sight be equated with an economic perspective that insists on the procedure and results of a calculation (Yuengert 2012, 57, 74–75; Hirschfeld 2018, 179). However, we observe that the Thomasian conception of prudence is close to its contemporary understanding, found for example in Kimball (1990). Indeed, the imprudence described here by Aquinas does not consist of an increase in *risk in general*, understood as an undifferentiated spread of probabilities, but of an increase in the *risk of loss*, understood this time as a spread of probabilities towards the lowest values. Imprudence can therefore be visualised by a leftward spread of the curve representing the probability density function.

This imprudence can occur at two levels: a lack of attention (*incaute*), which leads the merchant to make inappropriate expenditures out of negligence, and bad management (*imprudenter*), which leads the merchant to make inconsiderate expenditures, not out of negligence but out of bad anticipation, that is, incompetence, whereas the scholastic canonists intended the merchant to be prudent (*prudens*) in the sense of "competent" (Lemoine 1991, 30; Langholm 2003, 153, 163).

It is clear from *De emptione* that the merchant still faces two types of risk: first, he is subject to the fluctuation of prices on the market and does not know the price and quantities of the sale. Secondly, he cannot pass on all expenses in the price, since some of them may be illicit.

After having established the two categories of qualitative and quantitative risks in the *Commentary on the Sentences*, Aquinas makes a triple move in *De emptione*:

1. Aquinas addresses the quantitative dimension of justice by introducing the notion of price:
   (a) He distinguishes between licit and illicit expenses.
   (b) The ultimate licit expenditure is the one of transport.
   (c) The interest-bearing loan is illicit, even for financing a licit expenditure.
   (d) The determination of illicit expenditure leads Aquinas to distinguish two levels of merchants' imprudence. This leads Aquinas to an analysis of the merchant's care and skill.
   (e) The merchant must take responsibility for the consequences of his own care and skill.
2. He establishes a link between the qualitative and quantitative dimensions of justice, since the justice of the price depends on the prudence of the expenditure, and this prudence is both qualitative (amount of the expenditure) but, and more importantly, qualitative (nature of the expenditure).
3. He implicitly extends the treatment of exchange justice to both parties through the notion of price, which is an exchange ratio. We will have to wait until later writings such as *S. T.*, IIa IIae, q. 77, a. 1 to find an approach that explicitly deals with both parties, but here we find an implicit first step.

From these clarifications in *De emptione*, III on the treatment of trade, a number of risks emerge:[18]

First, there are analytical risks:

RTde1: A risk of error on the expenditure's licitness.

RTde2: A risk of error on the usefulness of business development.

[18] Risks on trade in *De emptione*, numbered "RTde".

RTde3: A risk of error on the licitness of the expenditure financing a licit expenditure (production and trade financing).

RTde4: A risk of error in identifying expenditure made without precaution.

RTde5: A risk of error in identifying expenditure made unwisely.

RTde6: A risk of error in identifying expenditure made without precaution.

The lack of information, at the time of expenditure, on the conditions of the sale, also entails commercial risks, which are not linked to the intention of co-contractors:

RTde7: Merchant's risk of transport (theft and shipwreck).

RTde8: Merchant's risk on the quantity sold due to the time gap, the evolution of the demand in the market, and ignorance of this price when he makes the expenditure.

RTde9: Merchant's risk on the selling price due to the time gap, the evolution of the price on the market and ignorance of this price at the time he makes the expenditure.

We can also highlight two strategic risks:

RTde10: Risk to the customer that the merchant passes off illicit expenditure as licit and includes it in the price.

RTde11: Risk for the merchant that the customer denounces licitly incurred expenses as illicit and that they are not included in the price whereas they should be included in the price.

The *Commentary on the Sentences* and *De emptione* thus offer a broad presentation of the risks incurred by agents in the course of commercial transactions. The *Commentary on the Sentences* offers a general framework presenting both a qualitative and quantitative structure of risk, whereas *De emptione* thinks of the justice of exchange more specifically in terms of price, introducing its lexicon and specifying its content. By clarifying the notion of fraud through an initial list of licit and illicit expenditures, Aquinas reduces the risk of analysis while clarifying the strategic risk. The introduction of the notion of price also clarifies the commercial risk as a price risk. The late works confirm this price approach to commercial activity. However, the contributions of the first two texts on this issue remain unique, on the one hand, because the framework laid down by the *Commentary on the Sentences* thereafter remains an implicit foundation, albeit without being taken up explicitly, and on the other hand because the approach to justice by the nature of the expenditure, addressed in *De emptione*, and more particularly by the notion of prudence, is no longer developed in the later works, although it underpins their statements on both the just price and usury.

Risks on Exchange Ratio

The strictly economic texts of the *Commentary on the Sentences* and *De emptione* show the importance of price as a criterion of justice in exchange. In order to identify the risks to this justice, it is therefore necessary to come back to what Aquinas means by a just price. The concept, not introduced in the economic texts but in the spiritual and theological texts, sheds light on three limit cases of exchange: the exchange between God and man, which takes place according to an exchange ratio that, in order to be just, cannot be a price; the exchange of a good which cannot be the object of a price, in this case the spiritual good on pain of the sin of simony; and the exchange of a good that is subject to a price but whose sale is also governed by a strong qualitative constraint that takes precedence over the possibility of a sale at a just price, in this case the married serf, who cannot be sold far away by the lord on pain of violating his marriage. The three cases mentioned by Aquinas raise a series of risks concerning the existence, nature and level of the exchange ratio.

The Advent of Just Price: Does God Give or Trade?

The first time the expression "just price" appears in Aquinas's works is in his commentary on the book of the prophet Isaiah (Januard 2025a). This student work, often seen as the first theological work by Aquinas, was probably written in Paris in 1252 and predates the *Commentary on the Sentences* (1254–1256) by a few years (Oliva 2006, 207–225; Torrell 2015, 53–54). Aquinas thus uses the notion of just price in his theological and spiritual texts before it appears in his economic texts. Although this first occurrence of the phrase is metaphorical, it nevertheless gives direction to Aquinas's concept of the just price in human and terrestrial exchanges, which he then puts into practice while shedding further light on our understanding of it. There are two paradoxes here. The first is that a technical expression often regarded as emblematic of Aquinas's contribution to economic thought should appear in a biblical commentary on a verse dealing with the spiritual relationship between God and human beings. The second, consistent with the first, is that Aquinas uses this expression, which evokes exchange according to a price, that is, with a counterpart of equal value, to comment on a biblical verse long received as representative of God's giving freely to humanity:

> All you who are thirsty, come to the waters, and you who have no money, make haste, buy and eat: come, buy without money and without exchange wine and milk. (*Vulgate*—Isaiah 55:1)

Aquinas comments on the verse as follows: "'come, buy', take as if you were buying, 'even without money', which is less than the just price [*idest minus quam justo pretio*]" (*Super Isaiam*, 55, 1). Aquinas defines the notion of "price" a few years later in the *Commentary on the Sentences*, considering that "the price of the purchase is given as a measure equivalent [*quasi mensura adaequans*] to what is purchased" (*In IV Sent.*, d. 25, q. 3, a. 2, qc. 1, resp.).

The passage needs to be placed in its theological context. Isaiah 55 follows shortly after the song of the Suffering Servant (Isaiah 52:13–53:12), recognised by Christian tradition and by Aquinas as the prefiguration of suffering Christ. The name "price" appears once in *Super Isaiam*, 52, but not to evoke the price represented by Christ's sacrifice. However, 20 years later, it appears 17 times in the treatise on the Passion in the *Summa theologiae* (*S. T.*, IIIa, q. 46–52) to evoke the redemption of humankind through the sacrifice of the Cross. According to its definition, the term "price" is used here to describe the only exchange between contributions of equal value that Aquinas could consider about God, since only the sacrifice of Christ is equal to the gift made by God. However, he does not use the expression "just price" on this occasion, since the immediate causes of the Passion, both of Isaiah's Suffering Servant and of Christ, relate rather to iniquity and wickedness. Considering now the nature and amount of the counterpart paid by man for the gift of wisdom, we must remember that it is a part of an exchange in which an offering of a different nature and on a different scale has already been made by Christ.

The first occurrence of "just price" reveals a risk concerning the nature of the transaction and a risk concerning the exchange ratio. The first risk concerns the nature of the transaction, since what appears at first sight to be a gift, and was considered as such until the beginning of the thirteenth century (Januard 2022a, 585–589), is treated by Aquinas as an exchange with a counterpart.

The Church Fathers favoured an interpretation in terms of a gift, although the idea of a commitment in return on the part of the recipient, rather than a counterpart, soon emerged. Aquinas marks a decisive stage with his interpretation in terms of exchange. Indeed, Jerome of Stridon (†420) comments on the verse by a double quotation, which certainly introduces a gift, but not a gift pure and simple, but one which requires a gift in return, or more precisely an extension of the initial gift (Jerome, *Super Isaiam*, col. 548): "By grace you have been saved" (Ephesian 2:8) and "you have received freely, give freely [*Gratis accepistis, gratis date*]" (Matthew 10:8). Like his predecessors, the ninth-century Latin theologian Haimo of Auxerre gives a spiritual-metaphorical interpretation of money, which for him represents eloquence (Haimo, *Super Isaiam*, col. 1000). He comments on the Gospel verse "you have received freely, give freely" (Matthew 10:8) by introducing, in the framework of a spiritual interpretation, a brief reference to an economic operation. He does not use the Ephesians quotation, however, which is more gift-oriented: although there is no commercial exchange, there must be reciprocity of gift, or rather a continuation of gift, because the final receiver is not the original giver, who is God. Haimo thus suggests a distinction between the order of exchange and the order of gift, the latter obtaining where there is neither exchange nor money. However, there is a counterpart in the sense of an obligation for a third party, since man must give in turn. The *Glossa Ordinaria* of the twelfth century insists on the difference between human wisdom, which can be bought for money in gold or silver, and divine wisdom, which cannot. Moreover, the *Glossa* criticises human money as false (*reprobum est*). The marginal gloss sets up a combined framework by taking up Jerome's combination of Ephesians 2:8 and Matthew 10:8 (*Glossa ordinaria*, III, Isaias, 55). Thus, at the end of the twelfth century, the understanding of Isaiah 55:1 remained the same as it was for Jerome, that is, a gift, but one which calls not exactly for a counterpart but for the propagation of the gift.

In the first half of the thirteenth century, a new understanding of the verse is offered by Hugh of Saint-Cher, the exegete and later Dominican cardinal with whom Albert the Great interceded in order to send his student Thomas Aquinas from Cologne to Paris in 1252 to teach, in spite of his young age (Weisheipl [1974] 1993, 64). Hugh comments: "buy, do not understand it as an exchange, in which money is paid [*emite, non intelligatis de commutatione, in qua appenditur argentum*], but only by the toil of the path [*sed pro laboris itineris tantum*]" (Hugh, *Postilla super Isaiam*,

c. 55, p. 130). Hugh is being innovative, thinking of a non-monetary exchange that is accessible to the poor who have no money. The counterpart here is man's effort on the path of a holy life and the hardship he endures. However, the gift framework is not entirely absent for Hugh: in his commentary on the book of Revelation, as part of a meditation on the free gift, which means a gift in the absence of merit, he quotes the entire verse but does not comment upon it (Hugh, *Super Apocalypsim*, c. 22, p. 429).

Albert the Great, under whom Aquinas was a biblical bachelor and perhaps wrote his *Super Isaiam*, also composed a *Commentary on the Book of Isaiah*, which was absent for a long time from classical editions and was included in the Cologne critical edition in 1952. The dating is uncertain, but it has been estimated as around 1250 (Siepmann and Simon 1952, XX). Money refers, as for Haimo, to eloquence: "Money means a ringing and resonating speech [*Argentum propter tinnulum sonum eloquium significant*]", Albert writes. He adds: "those who have no eloquence must nevertheless hasten to the doctrine and grace of the Lord [*Qui enim eloquentiam non habent, nihilominus properare debent ad doctrinam domini et gratiam*]" (Albert the Great, *Postilla super Isaiam*, c. 55, l. 26–32). It is thus a gift only in appearance, for this means that those who have eloquence must offer it as the counterpart, while the rest must make their way to divine grace: all must therefore do something in return for what seemed to be a gift. In this sense, Albert comments on "buy [*emite*]" by introducing an exchange: "by an exchange of merit in reward [*commutatione scilicet meriti in praemium*]" (l. 45–46). Then he comments on "without exchange": "we can exchange nothing because we have got nothing [*nihil enim commutare possumus, quia nihil habemus*]" (l. 51–52). Albert does not say that the transaction takes place outside the framework of exchange, but simply that man has nothing to exchange. The counterpart can thus tend towards zero or be zero, but the framework of analysis is still that of exchange, since the concept of a counterpart is introduced. A few lines above, the counterpart was even non-null since it was merit.

Aquinas takes a new step. He discusses the level of the exchange ratio relative to what would be the just price. The understanding in terms of an exchange with counterpart is confirmed in his later writings: the two times he comments on this biblical verse in his later works, he discusses what kind of counterpart this would be. The framework generated by the references to Isaiah 55:1 in Aquinas's work is that of a barter between divine wisdom, provided by God, and a counterpart, described later as study (*In Matthaeum*, c. 25, l. 1, n°2026) or eloquence (*In Joannem*, c. 6, l. 1, n°849), provided by people.

It is thus clear that the first risk that arises is whether the operation described is a gift or an exchange. The successive interpretations, and in particular the hesitations of the Fathers, who were unable to move beyond the framework of gift without recognising that it was absolutely gratuitous without any reciprocal commitment, clearly highlight this difficulty in conceptualising the operation, even before establishing the right amount of the consideration.

The second risk, which follows on from this, concerns the exchange ratio. The just ratio of exchange is not a price, since the transaction is carried out at "less than the just price", but it cannot be unjust since it is carried out by God, who does not commit injustice. The exchange ratio is not one of equality of thing to thing (*aequalitas rei*), as a price would be conceived according to commutative justice (*S. T.*, IIa IIae, q. 77, a. 1, ad 3). In *Super Isaiam*, 55, 1, the exchange ratio integrates the resources (non-monetary and limited) of the buyer, the human being, who could not pay the just price for a good of such great value (the grace of God), along with the will of the seller (God) that the exchange take place. The consideration must be of a currency and an amount that is available. The inaugural use of the expression "just price" thus paradoxically introduces exchanges that do not take place according to a price. It does, however, make it possible to deal with these limit cases within the framework of exchange, even though they do not fall under the heading of gift, since they involve an exchange ratio and a counterpart. This openness to a plurality of exchange ratios makes it possible to reduce the risk relating to the exchange ratio by providing a visible account of the justice of the exchange, even when this justice is not ensured by a price but by a "tariff", in the sense of Steiner and Trespeuch (2014), that is, a stipend that makes it possible to reproduce the transaction in the interests of society. Here, the stipend has a different role: it aims to involve the human being in the exchange. He is granted divine grace, but he must bring what he can in exchange in order to be part of the operation initiated by God. However, from an economic point of view, the framework is the same and can be used for other exchanges, in particular those which, as in *Super Isaiam*, 55, 1, concern a good or service for which the receiver cannot pay a counterpart of equal value.

The plurality of exchange ratios would later enable Aquinas to think of exchanges as consisting of a form of compensation rather than a payment of equal value. The closest case to *Super Isaiam* is the remuneration of the priest for the spiritual service he renders. He may receive a "kind of means of subsistence [*quasi sustentamentum vitae*]", but not "the price of the Mass [*pretium missae*]" (*In IV Sent.*, d. 25, q. 3, a. 2, qc. 1, ad 4); or a "stipend for the necessity [*stipendium necessitatis*]", but not "the price of a wage [*pretium mercedis*]" (*S. T.*, IIa IIae, q. 100, a. 2, resp.). This stipend enables him to continue his service, but Aquinas insists, for two reasons, that this is not a price: it is not a price of the Mass, taken as the sacrament coming from God, since grace conferred by the sacrament is unaffordable; and neither is it a price of a wage, since the nature of the cleric's service cannot be paid as any work. A similar situation, but more complex, is the case of the remuneration of the lawyer (*advocatus*), which, like that of the doctor (*medicus*), must be moderate and is not based solely on the equality of things, but is done "taking into account the personal condition [of their clients: *considerata conditione personarum*], the cases [handled: *negotiorum*], the work [*laboris*], and the customs of the country [*consuetudine patriae*]" (*S. T.*, IIae IIae, q. 71, a. 4, resp.). Here, as in *Super Isaiam*, the fair exchange ratio takes into account the resources of the buyer and is therefore not a price. Aquinas goes into more detail here, resulting in a multifactorial counterpart.

Other cases of exchange ratios that are not a price are loan interest and merchant's income. The diversity of exchange ratios and kinds of counterpart set up the first elements of the functional distinction between incomes. First, the loan cannot involve interest, because the compensation (*recompensatio*), or the amount of the sale of money, is the equal sum returned (*S. T.*, IIa IIae, q. 78, a. 1, ad 5 and a. 2, ad 4). It is a quantified counterpart, but the word used is not "price". Moreover, the loan can give rise to another kind of compensation: a gracious gift (*gratium donum*) or a non-financial compensation such as benevolence and love (*S. T.*, IIa IIae, q. 78, a. 2, resp. and ad 1). What is more, Aquinas gradually admits extrinsic titles: in *S. T.*, IIa IIae, q. 78, a. 2, ad 1, by stipulating compensation for the damage caused by the deprivation of the sum (*damnum emergens*), that is, the opportunity cost (but excluding *lucrum cessans*, loss of profit); and in *De malo*, q. 13, a. 4, ad 14, where Aquinas opens the way to *poena conventionalis*, a penalty for late repayment, by setting an *interesse*. This noun is used by canonists in the Middle Ages (McLaughlin 1939, 141; Blaise 1975, 499 gives Aquinas's *De malo* as the key reference) to indicate that the time gap has to be compensated (in contrast to the later meaning of the term "interest", this refers to the delay in payment, not to the interval between the loan and its due date).

Second, Aquinas distinguishes between the stipend or allowance (*stipendium*) which is the income of the soldier (*In IV Sent.*, d. 16, q. 4, a. 2, qc. 3, resp.) or of the merchant who transports and sells (*S. T.*, IIa IIae, q. 77, a. 4, resp.), and the wages (*praemium*) reserved for those who improve the good (*S. T.*, IIa IIae, q. 77, a. 4, ad 1). Although it rewards an effort (Koehler 2020, 362), the *stipendium* is a social compensation that allows the beneficiary to provide a service. In the case of the merchant, the service is the supply, but this compensation is not of a value equal to the work provided. On the other hand, in the case of improved goods, the increase in price reflects this improvement and results in a proportional *praemium* for the merchant-craftsman.

The plurality of exchange ratios makes it possible to ensure the continuity of an activity that cannot be priced or for which the use of a price, which would be inaccessible, would lead to its cessation. However, this leads to the emergence of a new type of risk. In addition to the traditional risks relating to the level of the price and its actual payment, there are now upstream risks relating to the nature of the transaction and its exchange ratio.

Aquinas helps to reduce the risk by adopting a very rich lexicon, with each exchange ratio having a specific name. However, on the one hand, the terms he uses are common Latin terms whose meaning is sometimes broad and lacking precise technical definition, and on the other hand, he offers little precision as to the meaning of these terms. Secondly, Aquinas does not provide any rules for determining the right exchange ratio for any type of good. Each case is specific, and knowledge of the nature of the good and the exchange ratio attached to it is assumed to be self-evident, or at least known. Determining the fair exchange ratio for a previously unknown good, or a good whose nature is disputed, may therefore be erroneous.

As soon as the expression "just price" is used for the first time by Aquinas, two sets of risks emerge:[19]

Risks on the nature of the operation:

RERsi1: A risk of misunderstanding between a gift and an exchange.

RERsi2: A risk on the determination of the receiver of the counterpart or the propagation of the gift.

RERsi3: A risk on the nature of the counterpart.

[19] Risks emerging on the exchange ratio in *Super Isaiam*, 55, 1, numbered "RERsi".

Risks on the exchange ratio:

RERsi4: A risk of lack of precision embodied by the name of the exchange ratio.

RERsi5: A risk that the exchange ratio is not affordable.

RERsi6: A risk that the currency is not available.

RERsi7: A risk on unfairness of the exchange ratio.

This founding text thus poses the fundamental question, which lies before all the others: Is the transaction an exchange or a gift? Then, if it is an exchange, it is necessary to determine the nature of the exchange ratio and the currency of the consideration. An error in the answer to one of these preliminary questions renders obsolete all the subsidiary questions, to which commentators are usually more attentive, such as the correct level of the price. This last question is only significant if the transaction is an exchange, and an exchange based on a price. *Super Isaiam* also highlights the need for the currency and the amount of the consideration to be affordable to the buyer if the transaction is to be completed.

The Risks of Buying and Selling on the Edge of the Trading Sphere

The next two instances of the expression "just price" are found in the *Commentary on the Sentences*. Surprisingly, they do not relate to economic issues such as usury (*In III Sent.*, d. 37, a. 6) or the activities of merchants (*In IV Sent.*, d. 16, q. 4, a. 2, qc. 3), but to the sacraments. The first one concerns simony, the sale of a spiritual good (*In IV Sent.*, d. 25, q. 3, a. 1, qc. 1), and the second the sale of a married serf (*In IV Sent.*, d. 36, q. 1, a. 2). These two terms are used to describe limit situations of exchange. It is not a case of exchange simply taking place according to a price, that is, with a counterpart of equal value.

Like the situation described in *Super Isaiam*, simony calls into question the very existence of a price: "If it is with respect to quantity [*in quantum*], then there is injustice [*injustitia*], as [*sicut cum*] when someone does not buy or sell at a just price [*non justo pretio*]; but if it is with respect to the object [*in quid*], as [*cum*] when he sells or buys what is not the object of a price [*quid non cadit sub pretio*], then it is the sin of the simoniac" (*In IV Sent.*, d. 25, q. 3, a. 1, qc. 1, resp.). Aquinas's text may give the impression of two parallel determinations of the justice of exchange, one *in quantum*, the other *in quid*; in fact, though, they are two stages ordered one after the other, for there can be no just price if there is no price.

We would be too quick to conclude that spiritual goods, since they do not have a price tag, cannot be exchanged and can only be given as an unrequited gift. This is not what Aquinas writes, and he specifies in the same question that the priest may receive a "kind of means of subsistence [*quasi sustentamentum vitae*]" (*In IV Sent.*, d. 25, q. 3, a. 2, qc. 1, ad 4). Spiritual goods, which cannot be priced under penalty of the sin of simony, however, cover two different situations. We can take up the distinction between the *professional* simony, the payment for a cleric's professional service, which is subject to progressive though tacit approval and regulation rather than condemnation, and the *proprietary* simony (trafficking in land, offices, relics and consecrated vessels) which is strictly forbidden (Ekelund et al. 1996, 32). Proprietary simony is a personal enrichment through the sale of that which did not really belong to the seller and which came from God or was consecrated to God, whereas professional simony consists in charging for a legitimate professional service that should be free because it confers spiritual goods.

To account for professional simony, which consists in assigning a price to the mass instead of sticking to a licit stipend, the approach of commodification studies is more relevant than a strict opposition between what may be commodified and what may not. In the way Aquinas deals with the exchange of spiritual goods such as the sacraments, we can note both *partial* commodification and *lexical* commodification (Januard and Lapidus 2023, 126–130). On the one hand, this does not mean that everything that isn't a commodity is a gift. The plurality of exchange ratios opened up by *Super Isaiam*, 55, 1 enables us to envisage the exchange of goods for which a price cannot be set, but for which a counterpart, not of equal value, can be provided. We can therefore speak of a form of partial commodification through the exchange with counterpart of what is not, however, the subject of a price. On the other hand, the qualitative impossibility of a just price is gradually expressed by Aquinas in the very terms of price in its quantitative dimension. Whereas the *Commentary on the Sentences* focuses on the expression "that which is not the object of a price" (*In IV Sent.*, d. 25, q. 3, a. 1, qc. 1, resp.), the *Summa theologiae* would evolve 15 years later to express the impossibility of a just price in terms of price level: "A spiritual thing cannot be compensated for by an earthly price [...] it is more precious than all riches [*cunctis opibus*]" (*S. T.*, IIa IIae, q. 100, a. 1, resp.), and "the Gospel cannot be sold [...]. That would be selling a great thing for a very low price" (*S. T.*, IIa IIae, q. 100, a. 3, ad 2). The mature works thus offer a form of lexical commodification, although this process is paradoxically intended to express the impossibility of a sale according to a price.

There are two kinds of risks in Aquinas's treatment of simony. First, Aquinas does not distinguish between the two forms of simony, that is, professional simony, which allows an exchange, and proprietary simony, for goods that are not exchangeable and for which no counterpart is allowed. He seems to only address professional simony and to place the distinction at the level of the existence of a price, and not of the possibility of exchange, which remains for professional simony even if this exchange is not carried out according to a price. Aquinas therefore does not address the total impossibility of exchange, that is, either the repatriation of the transaction within the free gift, or the impossibility of a gift or a loan, even without a counterpart. There is therefore, at least theoretically, a category of goods which can be understood in the sense of justice *in quid* proper to simony, but which Aquinas does not deal with explicitly: goods which are not only priceless but also non-exchangeable, or even non-transferable. There is thus a risk of confusion, within what has no price, between what can nevertheless be exchanged by means of another exchange ratio and what cannot.

Second, by clearly formulating the criterion of *quid* here, Aquinas clarifies what was still in abeyance in the *Super Isaiam*. It is indeed the nature of the good that determines the type of exchange ratio to which it can give rise (Januard 2023, 664–676; Januard 2025b). Aquinas here reduces the risk of employing other criteria that would not be relevant. He makes an objectivist shift, towards the justice of the operation as a reality external to the intention of the agents. Thomasian justice can certainly be seen from the perspective of agents (Koehn and Wilbratte 2012), since it is their behaviour that is right or wrong (Hamouda and Price 1997, 196–199) and this behaviour is relatively predictable in Thomasian anthropology (Conrad and Hunter 2020), but focusing on the good exchanged reduces what we could call an anthropological risk. However, no more than in *Super Isaiam* does he provide a general rule for characterising the *quid*. There therefore remains a risk of error as to the possibility of assigning a price to the good.

The second use of the expression "just price" in the *Commentary on the Sentences* occurs when Aquinas addresses the sale of the married serf. Aquinas never considers the serf as a "thing" but always as a human being, with full human dignity. Natural right, in this case, the right to sleep, eat or marry, therefore protects the serf, and Aquinas specifies that serfdom can only be partial and that obedience is only required in the execution of servile tasks (*S. T.*, IIa IIae, q. 104, a. 5, resp.). Although economically, the married serf is here considered as a commodity, which can be sold at a price and traded, this preliminary clarification remains fundamental. In addition, a serf could marry without his lord's permission, since marriage was a matter of divine and natural law, whereas serfdom was a matter of positive law (*In IV Sent.*, d. 36, q. 1, a. 2, resp.). Thus, a first risk emerges here for the lord. The serf's marriage has two potential consequences for the price, one upwards, the other downwards. Thus, it therefore represents what we would call today a positive and a negative pecuniary externality for the lord.

The upward pressure comes from the reproductive capacity that can possibly be offered by marriage. By marrying, the serf is a priori able to have children, thus providing the new owner with additional production capacity and reducing his average production costs. This should therefore put upward pressure on the just price. However, Aquinas points out in *In IV Sent.*, d. 36, q. 1, a. 4, resp. that the children tend to follow the status, and if necessary the lord, of their mother and not their father. Indeed, the offspring receive from their mothers the substance of their bodies, and servitude is a corporeal condition (on the evolution of the treatment of different cases in the Middle Ages, see Misserey 1931, note 14, 285–286). The increase of the just price by marriage would therefore be proper to the woman, not the man. Aquinas also mentions the practice in some countries of dividing children between the lords of each of the two serf parents, or of one lord buying them back from the other, but does not consider this reasonable. Thus, the positive pecuniary externality and the rise in the level of the just price would only occur in the case where the serf who marries is a woman.

The downward pressure comes from the geographical constraint through what we could call a criterion of market liquidity. Aquinas's article's *objectio* 4 (*In IV Sent.*, d. 36, q. 1, a. 2, obj. 4) upholds the obligation to ask the lord's consent, since otherwise the lord could sell the serf to "remote areas [*extraneas regiones*]". Aquinas does not reply concerning the lord's permission, as he answers this in the *respondeo*, but he replies that in such a case the lord "must be forced [*cogedus est*] not to sell his serf under these conditions [*taliter*, i.e. in remote areas], especially when [*praecipue cum*] he does not lack the possibility of selling his serf everywhere at a just price" (*In IV Sent.*, d. 36, q. 1, a. 2, ad 4). Everything here is trade-related, but the conditions for practicing trade activity are subordinated to higher principles, in this case, the natural law of marriage, which does not affect the price but rather the conditions of trade activity (not selling far away). If the prohibition on the lord selling his serf far away applies especially when (*praecipue cum*) he can sell him everywhere at a just price, or, in other words, when the market is liquid and he can sell his serf anywhere, then this implies that there may be situations where this is not the case. Aquinas's expression can be understood as a concessive proposition, in which case the lord can sell far away if he cannot find a buyer nearby. There is therefore no longer any constraint on the liquidity to be included in the price, and the marriage is neutral for the just price. Aquinas's formulation can also be understood as an absolute prohibition on selling far away, considering the expression "*praecipue* cum" as a rhetorical confirmation of this prohibition and not as a concession in case the lord cannot find a nearby buyer at the right price. This hypothesis seems more relevant. Indeed, marriage, being according to this hypothesis, an intangible natural right, is not negotiable in terms of price. In this case, it can be assumed that the restriction placed on the liquidity of the market by the addition of a geographical constraint reduces the price of the married serf by integrating this constraint into the price, since the buyer will also be subject to this constraint if he wishes to resell him.

It should be noted here that both of these assumptions relate to "*praecipue cum*", that is, the possibility of a removal of the geographical restriction of the sale, but not to the nature of the exchange ratio, which is a price, as Aquinas's turn of phrase indicates. The sale is therefore called for at a just price, since an exchange must be just. Marriage can influence the level of the just price, but it does not affect the nature of the exchange ratio. We are therefore not, as in *Super Isaiam*, 55, 1 or *In IV Sent.*, d. 25, q. 3, a. 1, qc. 1, concerned with cases where the exchange ratio is other than the price, nor in a situation where the type of exchange ratio could change, which would indicate that the single serf and the married serf would constitute two different goods. On the contrary, here, the qualitative criterion of justice, namely the geographic constraint, can affect the quantitative criterion, but only quantitatively, not in its nature.

Several risks thus emerge: first, the risk of misinterpreting the expression "*praecipue cum*", since two hypotheses can be supported, and there is a lack of precision of the permitted geographical area that excludes remote "*extraneas regiones*". Secondly, in the hypothesis of an absolute prohibition on selling far away, for not only could the constraint exert downward pressure on the price, since the buyer was buying a less-liquid good, but liquidity could become a qualitative constraint manifested by the absence of a buyer in absolute terms, or at least at a just price, in the acceptable geographical area. The lord therefore runs the risk of not being able to sell his serf or of having to sell him at less than the just price.

The case of the sale of the married serf introduces two complementary criteria of justice: a quantitative criterion, the price, and a qualitative criterion, the place of the sale. These two criteria are complementary rather than substitutes. The establishment of two criteria of justice leads to the establishment of two related risks. Injustice can occur in both qualitative and quantitative terms. The impossibility of reducing the criteria of justice by substitution makes it impossible to reduce the number of risks. In this case, liquidity risk and price risk cannot be reduced to each other and are cumulative.

The non-substitutability of these criteria of justice completes and frames in a new way the contributions made earlier in the *Commentary on the Sentences.* The triptych of general conditions of professional trading, *persona*, *tempus*, *modus*, set out in *IV Sent.*, d. 16, q. 4, a. 2, qc. 3, had already been completed by the diptych set up by the distinction between justice of object (*in quid*) and justice of quantity (*in quantum*) when Aquinas addressed non-tradable goods in *In* IV *Sent.*, d. 25, q. 3, a. 1, qc. 1. Here, he adds a criterion *locus* through the geographical restriction on the sale of the married serf.

Putting together the contributions of these three texts, each of which contributes to drawing up the framework for the justice of the exchange, a distinction can thus be made between qualitative and quantitative criteria. As we have seen, the qualitative criteria are *persona*, clerics and monks being excluded from professional trades; *tempus*, this activity being reserved for certain days; and the qualitative part of the *modus*. Indeed, the *modus* is "without fraud and according to a licit contract". Fraud may relate to the quality of the good or of the exchange, and the contract also provides for the non-financial terms of the exchange. To this must be added the *in quid* criterion which qualitatively determines the justice of the exchange according to the nature of the exchanged good. Finally, we here add the *locus* criterion, which determines the place of the sale according to the specific nature of the good. The quantitative criteria are the quantitative part of the *modus*, that is, fraud and the contractual dimension which affect the price, and the *in quantum* aspect of the justice of the exchange, when the possibility of a just price is not prevented by the nature of the good, that is, the justice *in quid*. We can therefore identify a set of qualitative criteria, *persona*, *tempus*, *modus*, *quid*, *locus*, and a quantitative criterion, which is the just price, in which the financial dimensions of the *modus*—that is, absence of fraud and respect for a licit contract—and justice *in quantum* are found.

Within the set of qualitative criteria for the justice of exchange, a first evolution towards an ontological approach can be noted. The specific nature of the non-tradable good, such as spiritual goods, and the semi-tradable good, such as the married serf, explicitly sets the limit of the trade activity according to a metaphysical delimitation made by reference to the good, as indicated by the criterion *in quid*. This delimitation, brought about directly by the treatment of simony and indirectly by the sale of the married serf through the criterion of *locus*, differs from the other conditions for three reasons. First, the original framework of *persona*, *tempus*, *modus* determines the fair terms of a certain kind of exchange, which is the professional trade of merchants; second, this triptych does not contain an *in quid* criteria related to the nature of the good exchanged; third, the introduction of the *in quid* criterion (including its variation in terms of *locus*) concerns the object of the exchange, and thus the very reason for trade.

There is a certain ontological reduction of qualitative criteria to the *quid*, which would tend to include the whole. In Aquinas's later works, such as the *Summa theologiae*, the *tempus* clause (days forbidden for trading) is less explicit. The *persona* clause (prohibition on clerics and monks) is found once, but reduced to clerics (*S. T.*, IIa IIae, q. 77, a. 4, ad 3), and the clause concerning the *modus* is present in the double dimension of the absence of fraud and respect for a licit contract at the beginning of the question on commercial exchange, but for goods which have obviously already been determined as being able to be exchanged according to a price:

> It is a sin to commit fraud in order to sell something for more than its just price [...] A contract must therefore be drawn up on the basis of equality of things between [the contracting parties]. (*S. T.*, IIa IIae, q. 77, a. 1, resp.)

With regard to usury, there are two clues in favour of a reduction to the *quid*. Firstly, in the *Commentary on the Sentences* Aquinas takes a step back from the traditional argument of *mutuum*, which concerns the nature of the loan, and therefore of the transaction, and structures a progressive argument centred on the nature of money, which is the thing exchanged

(*In III Sent.*, d. 37, a. 6, resp.; Januard 2021). Fifteen years later, attention to the *quid* can also be seen in the plan followed by the question on usury in the *Summa theologiae*, which shows the pre-eminence of the thing exchanged and then of the conditions of its exchange. The first article presents the nature of lending on the basis of the characteristics of money (*S. T.*, IIa IIae, q. 78, a. 1). Aquinas then turns, in a second article, to the modalities of compensation, which concern the relations between agents and even their reciprocal feelings: benevolence (*bonevolentiam*), friendship or love (*amorem*). However, Aquinas does not confine these relational compensations to pure subjectivity. They are merely a non-monetary consideration that the lender can demand (*exigere*). The third article deals with the nature of goods for which payment can be made for their use. The fourth and last article deals with the borrower's guilt, which causes the lender to sin if he pushes him to lend at interest, here approaching borrowing from a more subjective angle. The question on usury in the *Summa theologiae* thus confirms that the *quid* is central to the qualitative dimension of the justice of exchange.

We thus arrive at a model where the nature of the good exchanged dictates the nature of the exchange ratio, which dictates the attitude of the agents. This makes it possible to reduce the qualitative risk to the risk on the nature of the good and on the exchange ratio that this nature allows. It should be emphasised, however, that this model is only the result of a conceptual analysis of Thomasian writings, and Aquinas himself did not theorise about it. Moreover, this reduction to the *quid* remains partial, since some qualitative conditions of exchange still remain.

The additions made by the treatment of simony and the sale of married serfs therefore make it possible to identify new risks:[20]

Risks of misunderstanding

RERcs1: Risk of misunderstanding the reduction to the *quid*.

RERcs2: Risk of misunderstanding the non-substitutability of justice criteria.

RERcs3: Risk of an erroneous determination of the nature of the exchange ratio.

Operating risks

RERcs4: Risk of misidentifying the *quid*.

RERcs5: Risk of price (*in quantum*).

[20] Risks emerging on the exchange ratio in *the Commentary on the Sentences*, numbered "RERcs".

RERcs6: Risk of price induced by the qualitative constraint.

RERcs7: Risk of liquidity and on the possibility of selling due to the qualitative constraint.

The two occurrences of the expression "just price" in the *Commentary on the Sentences* make it possible to draw up an analytical model based on all the scattered elements from Aquinas's early texts. They suggest a series of risks that arise upstream of the transaction, at the time of determining what type of exchange can be applied to the property in question (Table 2.2).

Table 2.2 Risk mapping in Thomas Aquinas's early works

Reference	*Book*	*Text*
Risks on usury (RU)		
RUcs	*Commentary on the Sentences*	*III Sent.*, d. 37, a. 6
RUcs1: A reputational risk for the observer, if his analysis is wrong		
RUcs2: A reputational risk for the agent who is wrongly deemed to be a usurer because of the observer's erroneous analysis		
RUcs3: A risk to the borrower if the interest loan was wrongly authorised		
RUcs4: A risk to all agents, lenders and borrowers, who would have an interest in usury if it is wrongly prohibited		
RUcs5: A strategic risk for the lender that the borrower will take advantage of the risk of analytical error to make him look like a usurer		
RUcs6: A strategic risk for the borrower that the usurer will take advantage of the risk of analytical error to make his usurious activity look licit		
RUde	*De emptione*	*De emptione*, I, II, III, IV
RUde1: A risk that buyers and sellers in commercial operations may be involved in an usurious transaction		
RUde2: A risk that the buyer/borrower becomes a usurer if he asks for a discount that puts the price below the just price		
RUde3: A risk in the determination of the just price due to the fact that estimation is understood as an approximation		
RUde4: A risk of non-conformity of the actual price of the exchange with the value of the exchanged good when the value is translated into a price		
RUde5: An analysis risk on value due to a certain indeterminacy in this notion		
RUde6: An analysis risk on the role of the market as "just price taker" or "just price maker"		
Risks on trade (RT)		

(*continued*)

Table 2.2 (continued)

Reference	*Book*	*Text*
RTcs	*Commentary on the Sentences*	*IV Sent.*, d. 16, q. 4, a. 2, qc. 3
RTcs1: A risk in the understanding of commercial activity, as shown by the difference in position between Gratian and Peter Lombard on the one hand and Albert and Aquinas on the other hand		
RTcs2: A risk of subjective bias in the understanding of this activity, due to Aquinas's aristocratic background relative to the suspicious new social category of merchants		
RTcs3: A risk of scarcity because of Aquinas's emphasis on the justice of exchange rather than supply, although this need is perceived		
RTcs4: A risk on the just price and on the fair conditions of the exchange because of the general and relatively allusive nature of the notion of fraud		
RTcs5: A risk of shortage due to a halt in trade if the conditions imposed on merchants are disincentives through the notion of fraud		
RTcs6: A risk to the licitness of the activity		
RTcs7: A risk of remuneration, since the price has an upper bound by the notion of fraud but nothing protects the seller from an unfairly low price demanded by the buyer		
RTcs8: A risk that, even without fraud, the current price is not advantageous or that qualitative conditions are too restrictive		
RTcs9: A risk that, even without fraud, the current price or qualitative conditions are unfair by mistake		
RTcs10: A risk that the contract contains damaging errors		
RTcs11: A risk of fraud by the merchant		
RTcs12: A risk of the customer misrepresenting the merchant as a fraudster		
RTde	*De emptione*	*De emptione*, III
RTde1: A risk of error on the expenditure's licitness		
RTde2: A risk of error on the usefulness of business development		
RTde3: A risk of error on the licitness of the expenditure financing a licit expenditure (production and trade financing)		
RTde4: A risk of error in identifying expenditure made without precaution		
RTde5: A risk of error in identifying expenditure made unwisely		
RTde6: A risk of error in identifying expenditure made without precaution		
RTde7: Merchant's risk of transport (theft and shipwreck)		
RTde8: Merchant's risk on the quantity sold due to the time gap, the evolution of the demand on the market, and ignorance of this price when he makes expenditure		
RTde9: Merchant's risk on the selling price due to the time gap, the evolution of the price on the market and ignorance of this price at the time he makes the expenditure		
RTde10: Risk to the customer that the merchant passes off illicit expenditure as licit and includes it in the price		
RTde11: Risk for the merchant that the customer denounces licitly incurred expenses as illicit and that they are not included in the price whereas they should be included in the price		

(*continued*)

Table 2.2 (continued)

Reference	*Book*	*Text*
Risks on exchange ratio (RE)		
RERsi	*Super Isaiam*	*Super Isaiam*, 55, 1
RERsi1: A risk of misunderstanding between a gift and an exchange		
RERsi2: A risk on the determination of the receiver of the counterpart or the propagation of the gift		
RERsi3: A risk on the nature of the counterpart		
RERsi4: A risk of lack of precision embodied by the name of the exchange ratio		
RERsi5: A risk that the exchange ratio is not affordable		
RERsi6: A risk that the currency is not available		
RERsi7: A risk on unfairness of the exchange ratio		
RERcs	*Commentary on the Sentences*	*In IV Sent.*, d. 25, q. 3, a. 1, qc. 1 *In IV Sent.*, d. 36, q. 1, a. 2
RERcs1: Risk of misunderstanding the reduction to the *quid*		
RERcs2: Risk of misunderstanding the non-substitutability of justice criteria		
RERcs3: Risk of a wrong determining the nature of the exchange ratio		
RERcs4: Risk of misidentifying the quid		
RERcs5: Risk of price (*in quantum*)		
RERcs6: Risk of price induced by the qualitative constraint		
RERcs7: Risk of liquidity and on the possibility of selling due to the qualitative constraint		

References

Primary Sources

Albert the Great. 1891. *Ethicorum* [second commentary], ed. Borgnet, t. 7. Paris: Vivès.

———. 1893–1894. *In librum sententiarum*, ed. Borgnet, t. 25–30. Paris: Vivès.

———. 1952. *Postilla super Isaiam*, ed. Albertus-Magnus-Institut (Cologne), t. 19. Aschendorff: Monasterii Westfalorum.

———. 1968–1972. *Super Ethica* [first commentary], ed. Albertus-Magnus-Institut (Cologne), t. 14 (1). Aschendorff: Monasterii Westfalorum.

Aristotle. 1903. *Ethica Nicomachea*, editio altera, ed. Franciscus Susemihl, and Otto Apelt. Leipzig: Teubner.

———. 1970. *L'Éthique de Nicomaque*, introduction, traduction et commentaire par René Antoine Gauthier et Jean Yves Jolif, I, 2. Louvain: Publications Universitaires/Paris: Béatrice-Nauwelaerts.

———. [1938] 2002. *Rhétorique*, Livre II. Paris: Les belles lettres.
———. [1931] 2003. *Rhétorique*, Livre I. Paris: Les belles lettres.
Bernoulli, Jacob. 1713. *Ars conjectandi*, Basilae Impensis Thurnisiorum fratrum.
Biblia latina cum glossa ordinaria, III. 1992. Turnhout: Brepols.
Cicero. 1932. *Discours IX*. Paris: Les belles lettres.
———. 1940. *Caton l'Ancien*. Paris: Les belles lettres.
———. 1945. *Discours IV*. Paris: Les belles lettres.
Corpus Juris Canonici. 1661. Lyon: Laurent Anisson.
Corpus Juris Civilis. 1803. Metz/Paris: Behmer et Mamort/Rondonneau.
Giles of Lessines. 1875. *De usuris*. In Thomas Aquinas. *Opera Omnia*, t. 28. Paris: Vivès.
Gregory VII. 1853. *Concilium Romanum V*, in *Patrologiae cursus completus*, series Latina, t. 148. Paris: J.-P. Migne.
Haimo of Auxerre. 1879. *Commentariorum in Isaiam*. In Patrologiae cursus completes, series latina 116, col. 714–1086. Paris: Migne.
Hugh of Saint-Cher. 1645a. *Tomus quartum, in libors prophetarum*. Lyon: Societas Bibliopolarum.
———. 1645b. *Tomus septimus, Apocalypsim B. Ioannis*. Lyon: Societas Bibliopolarum.
Jerome of Stridon. 1865. *Commentariorum in Isaiam prophetam*. In Patrologiae cursus completes, series latina 24, col. 17–705. Paris: Migne.
Peter Lombard. 1916. *Libri IV sententiarum*, t. 1 and 2. Claras Aquas: Typis Collegii S. Bonaventurae, Quaracchi.
Robert of Courçon. 1902. In *De usura*, ed. Georges Lefèvre. Lille: Travaux et mémoires de l'Université de Lille.
Thomas Aquinas. 1863. *Postilla super Psalmos*, in Opera omnia, t. 14. Parme: P. Fiaccadori.
———. 1884. *Commentaria in octo libros physicorum Aristotelis*, ed. Leonina, t. 2. Rome: Typographia polyglotta S. C. de Propaganda Fide.
———. 1892. *Summa theologiae*, Ia IIae, qq. 71–114, ed. Leonina, t. 7. Rome: Typographia polyglotta S. C. de Propaganda Fide.
———. 1895. *Summa theologiae*, IIa IIae, qq. 1–51, ed. Leonina, t. 8. Rome: Typographia polyglotta S. C. de Propaganda Fide.
———. 1897. *Summa theologiae*, IIa IIae, qq. 52–122, ed. Leonina, t. 9. Rome: Typographia polyglotta S. C. de Propaganda Fide.
———. 1903. *Summa theologiae*, IIIa, qq. 1–59, ed. Leonina, t. 11. Rome: Typographia polyglotta S. C. de Propaganda Fide.
———. 1929–1947. *Scriptum super Sententiis*, 4 t. Paris: P. Lethielleux.
———. 1951. *Super Evangilium S. Matthaei lectura*, cura P. Raphaelis Cai. Rome: Marietti.
———. 1952. *Super Evangilium S. Joannis lectura*, cura P. Raphaelis Cai. Rome: Marietti.

———. 1953. *Catena aurea in quattuor Evangelia*. Rome: Marietti.

———. 1969. *Sententia libri Ethicorum*, ed. Leonina, t. 47. Rome: Commissio Leonina.

———. 1971. *Sententia libri Politicorum*, ed. Leonina, t. 48. Rome: Commissio Leonina.

———. 1974. *Expositio super Isaiam ad litteram*, ed. Leonina, t. 28. Rome: Santa Sabina.

———. 1976. *Quaestiones disputatae de veritate*, qq. 21–29, ed. Leonina, t. 22. Rome: Editori di San Tommaso.

———. 1979. *Opuscula III*, ed. Leonina, t. 42. Rome: Commission Leonina.

———. 1982. *Quaestiones disputatae de malo*, ed. Leonina, t. 23. Paris/Rome: Commissio Leonina—J. Vrin.

———. 1989. *Expositio libri posteriorum*, ed. Leonina, t. 1*2. Paris/Rome: Commissio Leonina—J. Vrin.

———. 1996. *Quaestiones de quolibet*, ed Leonina, t. 25.2. Paris/Rome: Commissio Leonina—ed. du Cerf.

William of Auxerre. 1980–1987. *Summa aurea*. Paris/Grottaferrata: ed. du Centre national de la recherche scientifique/Editiones Collegii S. Bonaventurae ad Claras Aquas.

Secondary References

Andreau, Jean. 1987. *La vie financière dans le monde romain. Les métiers de manieurs d'argent (IVè siècle av. J.-C.—IIIè siècle ap. J.-C.)* (Bibliothèque des Écoles françaises d'Athènes et de Rome, 265). Rome: École française de Rome.

———. 2000. Les intérêts des prêts dans les tablettes de Murecine. *Cahiers du Centre Gustave Glotz* 11: 151–159.

Baldwin, John W. 1959. The Medieval Theories of the Just Price. *Transactions of the American Philosophical Society* 49 (4): 1–92.

Bartell, Ernest. 1962. Value, Price, and St. Thomas. *The Thomist* 25 (3): 325–381.

Blaise, Albert. 1954. *Dictionnaire latin-français des auteurs chrétiens*. Strasbourg: ed. Le latin chrétien.

———. 1975. *Lexicon latinitatis Medii Aevi*. Turnhout: Brepols.

Bovon, François. 1991. *L'évangile selon saint Luc (1,1–9,50)*. Geneva: Labor et Fides.

Bréban, Laurie, and André Lapidus. 2019. Adam Smith on Lotteries: An Interpretation and Formal Restatement. *European Journal of the History of Economic Thought* 26 (1): 157–197.

Burke, Joseph A. 2014. The Scholastic Analysis of ZIRP: Justice, Usury, and the Zero Interest Rate Policy. *Journal of Markets & Morality* 17 (1): 105–124.

Byrne, Edmund. 1968. *Probability and Opinion: A Study in the Medieval Presuppositions of Post Medieval Theories of Probability*. The Hague: Martinus Nijhoff.

Ceccarelli, Giovanni. 1999. Le jeu comme contrat et le risicum chez Olivi. In *Pierre de Jean Olivi (1248–1298), pensée, scolastique, dissidence spirituelle et société*, ed. Alain Boureau and Sylvain Piron, 239–250. Paris: Vrin.

Ceccarelli, Giovanni, and Sylvain Piron. 2009. Gerald Odonis' Economics Treatise. *Vivarium* 147 (2–3): 164–204.

Chaplygina, Irina, and André Lapidus. 2016. Economic Thought in Scholasticism: Some Landmarks on Price and Interest. In *Handbook on the History of Economic Analysis*, ed. Gilbert Faccarello and Heinz D. Kurz, vol. II, 20–42. Cheltenham and Northampton: Edward Elgar.

———. 2022. Theorizing Interest: How Did It All Begin? Some Landmarks on the Prohibition of Usury in Scholastic Economic Thought. In *European and Chinese Histories of Economic Thought*, ed. Iwo Amelung and Bertram Schefold, 93–105. London: Routledge.

Cimma, Maria Rosa. 1984. *De non numerata pecunia*. Milan: A. Giuffrè.

Conrad, Richard, and Peter Hunter. 2020. Why Aquinas Would Agree that Human Economic Behaviour is Largely Predictable. In *Agency and Causal Explanation in Economics*, Virtues and Economics, ed. Peter Róna and László Zsolnai, vol. 5, 93–113. Cham: Springer.

Daston, Lorraine. 1988. *Classical Probability in the Enlightenment*. Princeton: Princeton University Press.

Daubercies, Pierre. 1990. Prudence. In *Catholicisme*, t. 13. Paris: Letouzé et Ané, col. 158–171.

De Roover, Raymond. 1946. Le contrat de change depuis la fin du treizième siècle jusqu'au début du dix-septième. *Revue Belge de Philologie et d'Histoire* 25 (1–2): 111–128.

———. 1953. *L'évolution de la lettre de change*. Paris: Librairie Armand Colin.

———. 1958. The Concept of the Just Price: Theory and Economic Policy. *Journal of Economic History* 18 (4): 418–434.

———. 1971. *La Pensée économique des scolastiques*. Montréal/Paris: Vrin.

Dellemotte, Jean. 2017. *Histoire des idées économiques*. Paris: Dunod.

Dempsey, Bernard W. 1935. Just Price in a Functional Economy. *American Economic Review* 25 (4): 471–486.

Dondaine, Hyacinthe-François. 1979. Préface. In Thomas d'Aquin, *De emptione et venditione ad tempus, Opuscula III*, ed. Leonina, t. 42, 381–390. Rome: Commissio Leonina.

du Passage, Henri. 1946. Usure. *Dictionnaire de théologie catholique*, t. 15. Paris: Letouzey et Ané, col. 2316–2390.

Dupuy, Claude. 1992. De la monnaie publique à la monnaie privée au bas Moyen Âge (XIIIe et XIVe siècles). *Genèses* 8: 25–59.

Ege, Ragip. 2014. La question de l'interdiction de l'intérêt dans l'histoire européenne. *Revue Économique* 65 (2): 391–419.

Ekelund, Robert B., Robert F. Hébert, et al. 1996. Sacred Trust. In *The Medieval Church as an Economic Firm*. New York/Oxford: Oxford University Press.

Ellul, Jacques. 2013. *Histoire des institutions. Le Moyen Âge*. Paris: Presses Universitaires de France.

Ernout, Alfred, and Antoine Meillet. 2001. *Dictionnaire étymologique de la langue latine*, 4th edition revised. Paris: Klincksieck.

Feller, Laurent. 2020. Les écritures de l'économie au Moyen Âge. *Revue Historique* 693: 25–65.

Feuvrier-Prévotat, Claire. 1993. Vocabulaire et statut de l'argent dans le théâtre de Plaute. In *Mélanges Pierre Lévêque*, Annales littéraires de l'Université de Besançon, 491, t. 7, 133–153.

Franks, Christopher A. 2009. *He Became Poor*. Cambridge: William B. Eerdmans Publishing Company.

Friedman, David. 1980. In Defense of Thomas Aquinas and the Just Price. *History of Political Economy* 12 (2): 234–242.

Gardin-Dumesnil, Jean-Baptiste. 1788. *Synonymes Latins*. Paris: Nyon le jeune.

Giliberti, Giuseppe. 1999. De la rente agricole à l'investissement financier: le rôle de l'esclave kalendario praepositus. *Topoi* 9 (1): 165–178.

Hacking, Ian. 2006. *The Emergence of Probability*. 2nd ed. Cambridge: Cambridge University Press.

Hamouda, Omar, and Betsey Price. 1997. The Justice of the Just Price. *European Journal of the History of Economic Thought* 4 (2): 191–216.

Hirschfeld, Mary L. 2018. *Aquinas and the Market*. Cambridge: Harvard University Press.

Hollander, Samuel. 1965. On the Interpretation of the Just Price. *Kyklos* 18: 615–634.

Imbach, Ruedi, and Adriano Oliva. 2009. *La philosophie de Thomas d'Aquin*. Paris: Vrin.

Januard, Pierre. 2021. Analysis Risk and Commercial Risk: The First Treatment of Usury in Thomas Aquinas's *Commentary on the Sentences*. *European Journal of the History of Economic Thought* 28 (4): 599–534.

———. 2022a. De l'*œconomia* à l'échange volontaire: la délimitation de l'activité économique chez Thomas d'Aquin. *Revue des Sciences Philosophiques et Théologiques* 106 (4): 567–609.

———. 2022b. Licit and Illicit Risks in Thomas Aquinas's *De emptione et venditione ad tempus*. *Œconomia* 12 (2): 233–271.

———. 2022c. Risks on Trade: The Activity of the Merchant in Thomas Aquinas's *Commentary on the Sentences*. *History of Economic Ideas* XXX (1): 47–98.

———. 2022d. Risky Exchanges: Price and Justice in Thomas Aquinas's *De emptione et venditione ad tempus*. *European Journal of the History of Economic Thought* 29 (4): 729–769.

———. 2023. Chose, activité, agents: Le regard novateur de Thomas d'Aquin sur les opérations économiques. *Revue des Sciences Philosophiques et Théologiques* 107 (4): 641–679.

———. 2024a. Probability, Prudence, Danger: Thomas Aquinas on the Building of the Lexicon of Risk. *Journal of the History of Economic Thought* 46 (3): 421–442.

———. 2024b. Production et échange chez Thomas d'Aquin: L'homme participe-t-il à l'œuvre de création? *Revue des Sciences Philosophiques et Théologiques* 108 (3): 499–533.

———. 2025a. Is God Giving or Trading: Thomas Aquinas's First Use of 'Just Price'. *History of Political Economy*, forthcoming.

———. 2025b. Thomas Aquinas's ontological approach to economic activity. In *Aquinas, Natural Law, and Social Ontology: Historical and Contemporary Perspectives*, ed. Ana Marta González. London: Routledge, forthcoming.

Januard, Pierre, and André Lapidus. 2023. Trading for No Price, Thomas Aquinas on Money Loans, Sacraments and Exchange. In *The Routledge Handbook of Commodification*, ed. Élodie Bertrand and Vida Panitch, 120–133. London: Routledge.

Kaplan, Steven Laurence. 1984. *Provisioning Paris, Merchants and Millers in the Grain and Flour Trade During the Eighteenth Century*. Ithaca and London: Cornell University Press.

Kaye, Joel. [1998] 2004. *Economy and Nature in the Fourteenth Century*. Cambridge: Cambridge University Press.

Kimball, Miles S. 1990. Precautionary Saving in the Small and in the Large. *Econometrica* 58 (1): 53–73.

Kirshner, Julius, and Kimberly Lo Prete. 1984. Peter John Olivi's Treatises on Contract of Sale, Usury and Restitution: Minorite Economics or Minor Works? *Quaderni Fiorentini per la Storia del Pensiero Giuridico Moderno* 13: 233–286.

Koehler, Benedikt. 2020. Thomas Aquinas on the Conduct of Sales. *Economic Affairs* 40: 358–366.

Koehn, Daryl, and Barry Wilbratte. 2012. In Defense of a Thomistic Concept of the Just Price. *Business Ethics Quarterly* 22 (3): 501–526.

Kübel, Whilelmus. 1968–1972. Prolegomena. In Albert le Grand, *Super Ethica*, ed. Albertus-Magnus-Institut (Cologne), t. 14 (1). Aschendorff: Monasterii Westfalorum, V–XVI.

Langholm, Odd. 1984. *The Aristotelian Analysis of Usury*. Bergen and Oslo: Universitersforlaget AS.

———. 1992. Economics in the Medieval Schools. In *Wealth, Exchange, Value, Money and Usury According to the Paris Theological Tradition, 1200–1350* (Studien und Texte zur Geistesgeschichte des Mittelalters, 29). Leiden: Brill.

———. 1998. *The Legacy of Scholasticism in Economic Thought, Antecedents of Choice and Power*. Cambridge: Cambridge University Press.

———. 2003. *The Merchant in the Confessional*. Leiden: Brill.

Lapidus, André. 1986. *Le détour de valeur*. Paris: Economica.

———. 1987. La propriété de la monnaie: doctrine de l'usure et théorie de l'intérêt. *Revue Économique* 38 (6): 1095–1109.

———. 1991. Information and Risk in the Medieval Doctrine of Usury during the Thirteenth Century. In *Perspectives on the History of Economic Thought*, ed. William Barber, vol. 5, 23–38. London: Edward Elgar.

———. 1992. Une introduction à la pensée économique médiévale. In *Nouvelle histoire de la pensée économique*, ed. Alain Béraud et al., vol. 1, 24–70. Paris: La Découverte.

———. 1994. Norm, Virtue and Information: Individual Behaviour and the Just Price in Thomas Aquinas' *Summa Theologiae. European Journal of the History of Economic Thought* 1 (3): 435–473.

———. 2021. Le prêt à intérêt face à la religion et au droit: imbrication et séparation aux premiers moments d'une histoire longue. In *La science des mœurs: de la conception à l'expérimentation*, ed. Laurie Bréban, Séverine Denieul, and Élise Sultan, 87–116. Paris: Garnier.

Le Goff, Jacques. 1986. *La bourse et la vie, économie et religion au Moyen Âge*. Paris: Hachette.

———. [1956] 2001. *Marchands et banquiers du Moyen Âge*. Paris: Presses Universitaires de France.

———. [2010] 2019. *Le Moyen Âge et l'argent, essai d'anthropologie historique*. Paris: Perrin.

Lemoine, Bernadette. 1991. La prudence chez saint Thomas d'Aquin: La problématique thomiste au regard de la philosophie aristotélicienne. Pour une relecture contemporaine du traité. *Divus Thomas* 94: 27–51.

Lupton, Sylvie. 2015. Quality Uncertainty in Early Economic Thought. *History of Political Economy* 47 (3): 511–534.

Mandonnet, Pierre. 1910. *Des écrits authentiques de s. Thomas d'Aquin*, 2nd edition revised. Fribourg: Imprimerie de l'œuvre de Saint-Paul.

McLaughlin, Terence P. 1939. The Teaching of the Canonists on Usury (1). *Mediaeval Studies* 1: 81–147.

———. 1940. The Teaching of the Canonists on Usury (2). *Mediaeval Studies* 2: 1–22.

Mélitz, Jacques. 1971. Some Further Reassessment of the Scholastic Doctrine of Usury. *Kyklos* 24: 473–492.

Misserey, Louis. 1931. Appendice I notes explicatives. In Thomas Aquinas, *Somme théologique*, le mariage, tome deuxième, Sup. q. 50–60, édition de la Revue des jeunes. Paris/Tournay/Rome: Desclée et Cie.

Monsalve, Fabio. 2014a. Scholastic Just Price Versus Current Market Price: Is it Merely a Matter of Labelling? *European Journal of the History of Economic Thought* 21 (1): 4–20.

———. 2014b. Late Spanish Doctors on Usury, and the Evolving Scholastic Tradition. *Journal of the History of Economic Thought* 36 (2): 215–235.

Munro, John H. 2003. The Medieval Origins of the Financial Revolution: Usury, *Rentes*, and Negotiability. *The International History Review* 25 (3): 505–562.

Nadjo, Léon. 1989. *L'argent et les affaires à Rome, des origines au IIe siècle avant J.-C., étude d'un vocabulaire technique*. Leuven/Paris: Peeters.

Noell, Edd S. 1998. Bargaining, Consent and the Just Wage in the Sources of Scholastic Economic Thought. *Journal of the History of Economic Thought* 20 (4): 467–478.

Noonan, John Thomas. 1957. *The Scholastic Analysis of Usury*. Cambridge: Harvard University Press.

O'Brien, George. [1920] 2001. *An Essay on the Mediaeval Economic Teaching*. Kitchener, Batoche Books.

O'Rahilly, Alfred. 1928. Notes on St. Thomas III—St. Thomas on Credit. *Irish Ecclesiastical Record*, 5th series 31: 159–168.

Oliva, Adriano. 2006. *Les débuts de l'enseignement de Thomas d'Aquin et sa conception de la Sacra doctrina*. Paris: Vrin.

Persson, Karl Gunnar. 2014. Markets and Coercion in Medieval Europe. In *The Cambridge History of Capitalism*, The Rise of Capitalism: From Ancient Origins to 1848, ed. Larry Neal and Jeffrey G. Willimson, vol. 1, 225–266. Cambridge: Cambridge University Press.

Piron, Sylvain. 1997. Marchands et confesseurs. Le Traité des contrats d'Olivi dans son contexte (Narbonne, fin XIIIe-début XIVe siècle). In *L'argent au Moyen Âge*, Actes des congrès de la Société des historiens médiévistes de l'enseignement supérieur public, 28e congrès, 289–308. Clermont-Ferrand.

———. 2012. Présentation: Contextes intellectuels et sociaux du Traités des contrats. In Pierre de Jean Olivi, *Traité des contrats*, ed. Sylvain Piron, 27–71. Paris: Les belles lettres.

Porro, Pasquale. 2015. *Thomas Aquinas. A Historical and Philosophical Profile*. Washington, DC: The Catholic University of America Press.

Quicherat, Louis. 1893. *Thesaurus poeticus linguae latinae*. Paris: Librairie Hachette et Cie.

Rajapakse, Nadeera. 2010. *L'intérêt: le juste prix de la monnaie*. Thèse soutenue pour le doctorat en sciences économiques. Paris: Université Paris 1 Panthéon-Sorbonne.

Rocha, Manuel. 1933. *Travail et salaire à travers la scolastique*. Paris: Desclée de Brouwer et Cie.

Santori, Paolo. 2020. *Donum*, Exchange and Common Good in Aquinas: The Dawn of Civil Economy. *European Journal of the History of Economic Thought* 27 (3): 276–297.

———. 2021. *Thomas Aquinas and the Civil Economy Tradition*. Abingdon/New York: Routledge.

Schuessler, Rudolf. 2019. *The Debate on Probable Opinions in the Scholastic Tradition*. Leiden: Brill.

Schumpeter, Joseph A. [1954] 2006. *History of Economic Analysis.* London: Routledge.

Schürmann, Heinz. 1983. *Il Vangelo di Luca. Parte prima.* Brescia: Paideia editrice.

Siepmann, Fernandus and Simon, Paulus. 1952. Prolegomena, in Albert le Grand, *Postilla super Isaiam*, ed. Albertus-Magnus-Institut, t. 19, Aschendorff: Monasterii Westfalorum, VII–XXII.

Sivéry, Gérard. 2004. La notion économique de l'usure selon saint Thomas d'Aquin. *Revue du Nord* 2004 (4): 697–708.

Spicq, Ceslas. 1935. Appendice I: notes explicatives. In Thomas Aquinas, *Somme Théologique*, Traité de la Justice, t. 3. Paris: Éditions de la Revue des Jeunes, 257–358.

Steiner, Philippe, and Marie Trespeuch. 2014. Introduction. In *Marchés contestés. Quand le marché rencontre la morale*, ed. Philippe Steiner and Marie Trespeuch, 7–27. Toulouse: Presses Universitaires du Midi.

Sturn, Richard. 2017. Agency, Exchange, and Power in Scholastic Thought. *European Journal of the History of Economic Thought* 24 (4): 640–669.

Synan, Edward A. 1988. St. Thomas Aquinas and the Profession of Arms. *Mediaeval Studies* 50: 404–437.

Tawney, Richard Henry. [1926] 1948. *Religion and the Rise of Capitalism.* London: John Murray.

Todeschini, Giacomo. 2012. Usury in Christian Middle Ages, A Reconsideration of the Historiographical Tradition (1949–2010). In *Religione e istituzioni religiose nell'economia europea, 1000–1800*, ed. Francesco Ammannati, 119–130. Florence: Firenze University Press.

Toivanen, Juhana. 2016. Voluntarist Anthropology in Peter of John Olivi's *De Contractibus. Franciscan Studies* 74: 41–65.

Torrell, Jean-Pierre. 2015. *Initiation à Saint Thomas d'Aquin*, nouvelle édition. Paris: Cerf.

Verdon, Jean. 2016. *S'amuser au Moyen Âge.* Paris: Tallandier.

Weisheipl, James A. [1974] 1993. *Frère Thomas d'Aquin.* Paris: Cerf.

Wirth, Jean. 1983. La naissance du concept de croyance. *Bibliothèque d'Humanisme et Renaissance* 45 (1): 7–58.

Worland, Stephen T. 1977. *Justum Pretium*, One More Round in an 'Endless Series'. *History of Political Economy* 9 (4): 504–521.

Wyffels, Carlos. 1991. L'usure en Flandre au XIIIe siècle. *Revue Belge de Philologie et d'Histoire* 69 (4): 853–871.

Yuengert, Andrew M. 2012. *Approximating Prudence.* New York: Palgrave Macmillan.

CHAPTER 3

Drawing Typologies and a Dynamic Structure of Risks

Abstract The risk mapping derived from the various economic activities presented by Thomas Aquinas enables the development of different typologies, which can then be cross-referenced with one another. Risk can be classified according to activity, such as loan, commercial exchange or limit cases of market exchange; according to whether it is a quantitative or qualitative risk; according to whether it is an error in understanding the transaction, a commercial risk imposed by external conditions on the co-contractors, or a strategic risk, which is an internal risk arising from the lack of information on the co-contractor's intention. They can also be distinguished according to whether the risk relates to the licitness of the activity, the conditions under which it is carried out or a remuneration risk. Finally, a distinction must be made between risks explicitly named by Aquinas, risks implicitly deducible from the situation described and risks induced by Aquinas's treatment of the situation. This approach reveals a dynamic structure of risk in Aquinas's thought, with risks emerging both upstream of the operation—concerning the nature of the activity and the nature of the good exchanged—and during the operation itself, involving a range of additional risks.

Keywords Risk typology • Usury • Just price • Risk • Exchange ratio • Probability • Danger • Prudence

P. Januard, *Thomas Aquinas on Risk in Economic Activity*,
https://doi.org/10.1007/978-3-031-83825-5_3

Introduction

A reading of the early writings on economics makes it possible to identify a range of risks and to map them out text by text, depending on whether they are presented in relation to usury, the activities of merchants, forward sales—which potentially relate to these two activities—or whether they appear in connection with the use of the expression "just price". This makes it possible to identify two sets of risk *typologies*. The first set is based on a classification of risks supported by economic analysis. Risks can thus be classified according to the *activity* in which they arise and their qualitative or quantitative *nature*, but also by *type* (analysis risk, commercial risk, strategic risk). A second set, based on a more distanced and broader reading of these writings and using the analytical framework employed by Aquinas in the rest of his work, makes it possible to analyse and break down the just price according to its *level of reality* on the basis of the philosophical concepts of *analogy* and *sign*, and to draw up a typology by *extension* (risks explicitly named by Aquinas, risks implicitly deducible from the situation described, and risks induced by the way in which Aquinas treats the situation). We can thus draw up a dynamic structure of risks as they appear in the early writings, starting with the risks that arise upstream of the exchange, characterising the risks in the exchange, and then identifying new risks that arise upstream of the exchange but only appear through the exchange.

From Mapping to Typology: Towards an Economic Analysis of Thomasian Risks

Risk mapping enables risks to be analysed according to economic criteria. The first step is to determine the type of *activity* in which they arise. We can thus classify activities according to a progression ranging from monetary lending to the limit cases of commercial exchange. Risks can also affect the *quantitative* dimension (price) or all the *qualitative* criteria of the justice of exchange. It is therefore possible to cross-reference these two typologies. Secondly, the risk may be one of *analysis*, since there may be a misunderstanding of the economic activity. This is the risk of the analyst, in the Middle Ages, the moralist, but it also affects the co-contractors. In this case, it is *commercial* risk, that is, a risk that comes from outside the exchange and is imposed on everyone, such as the general conditions on the market or the legal framework within which the activity is carried out.

Finally, agents may be exposed to a *strategic* risk, since their co-contractor may take advantage of an asymmetry of information in his favour. The agent is unaware of his co-contractor's intentions, which remain hidden. These three *types* of risk can be crossed with *levels* of risk: for example, for the merchant's activity, there is a risk concerning the licitness of his activity, a risk concerning the conditions of this activity and a risk concerning his remuneration.

Mapping Risks According to Economic Activities and the Nature of Risks

The text-by-text mapping enables us to carry out an initial classification of risks according to the activity in which they are involved, placing them along a *continuum* ranging from monetary lending to limit cases of commercial exchange, via forward sales, which seem to be part trade and part loan, and commercial activity proper. We can cross-reference this initial classification with a second, based on the most immediate approach to the nature of the risks, that is, whether they are qualitative or quantitative. Thus, we can obtain an initial cross-classification (Table 3.1):

The point here is to specify the nature of the risks and relate them to the economic situations described by Aquinas, depending on whether these situations are more akin to lending or commercial exchange.

The *quantitative* risk is that the transaction is carried out according to an exchange ratio whose level is unfair. This risk can be broken down into *instantaneous* and *intertemporal* risks:

Instantaneous risk is the most immediate. In the case of a monetary loan, this occurs if the sum returned differs from the sum lent (*In III Sent.*, d. 37, a. 6); in the case of a forward sale, if the price charged differs from that charged for a spot sale because of a credit charge (*De emptione*); in the case of trade, if the estimate of the just price is an erroneous approximation (*De emptione*, I), or if illicit expenses are reflected in the price (*De emptione*, III) and the sale is not made "without fraud and according to a licit contract" (*In IV Sent.*, d. 16, q. 4, a. 2, qc. 3); and in limit cases of exchange, if the error in the nature of the exchange ratio leads to a quantitative difference, due to the integration of other variables, between the ratio wrongly applied and the one which would be just (*Super Isaiam*, 55, 1; *In IV Sent.*, d. 25, q. 3, a. 1, qc. 1).

Intertemporal risks arise from the time lag between two transactions or two phases of the same transaction: Aquinas does not envisage a default in

Table 3.1 Quantitative and qualitative risks on economic activities

	← Usury	*Economic activity*		*Exchange →*
Activity *Risk*	*Monetary loans*	*Forward sales*	*Trade*	*Limit cases of exchange*
Quantitative risks				
Instantaneous risks	Gap between lent and repaid amount RUcs4–6[a]	Gap between spot and forward prices because of time Discount requested by the buyer for early payment RUde2	Estimation of the just price RTcs11 RTde1–11	Calculation of the exchange ratio Quantitative gap between price and stipend Price lowered by qualitative constraints RERsi7 RERcs5
Intertemporal risks	(Late repayment)[b]	(Default not mentioned)	Time gap between expenses and sales: need to forecast quantity and selling price RTde8–9	Time gap between expenses and sales: quantitative constraints on price may occur RERcs5
Qualitative risks				
Risks in determining criteria of justice	Analysis of *mutuum* and money RUcs1–6	Usury situation for the seller or the buyer RUde1–6	Justice criterion on the merchant activity (person, time, mode) Licit or illicit nature of expenses RTde1–11	Nature of the exchange ratio commanded by the good Qualitative constraint on the sale RERsi1–7 RERcs1–4; 6–7

(*continued*)

Table 3.1 (continued)

	← *Usury*	*Economic activity*		*Exchange* →
Activity Risk	*Monetary loans*	*Forward sales*	*Trade*	*Limit cases of exchange*
Risks in implementing criteria of justice	(Calculation method for compensation by extrinsic titles)	Approximation of the just price on the common market RUde3	Error on the person, the timetable, the fraud assessment and the contractualisation RTcs1–12	Error in the evaluation of the variables and their weightings in the calculation of the exchange ratio RERsi1–7 RERcs1–7

[a] This classification refers to risk mapping, see Chap. 2

[b] In comas: risks occurring in Aquinas's later works

payment for goods purchased on credit (*De emptione*), nor an absolute default in repayment of the loan (*In III Sent.*, d. 37, a. 6), but he suggests in his later works the possibility of a delay in repayment (*De malo*, q. 13, a. 4, ad 14). Moreover, in discussing the recovery of expenses in the sale price, he implicitly suggests the existence of a risk, even when the expense is licit and recoverable, since it is made without knowing with certainty the quantity that will be sold or the current market price at the time of the sale (*De emptione*, III). Similarly, in the limit case of the sale of a married serf, when the lord buys the serf, he has no knowledge of a possible future marriage, nor of what the market conditions will be in the vicinity when he plans to sell him (*In IV Sent.*, d. 36, q. 1, a. 2). To these situations must be added the fact that the agent may adapt his behaviour during the course of the exchange, which takes place over time. For example, in the case of a forward sale, the buyer may, between the time of the sale and the expected time of payment, come and demand a discount for early payment, and thus find himself in a situation of usury. This represents a risk of reduced turnover for the seller (*De emptione*, I).

The *qualitative risk* may be a risk of error in the understanding of the transaction, which may lead to an incorrect determination of the justice of criteria for the exchange, and a risk of implementation of the criteria of justice during the exchange:

The *risk of error* in the transaction may relate to the understanding of the loan as a *mutuum*, or of money as fungible during the course of the loan (*In III Sent.*, d. 37, a. 6; Januard 2021, 611–621; Januard 2024a, 425–430); it may relate, in the case of forward sales, to the characterisation of the situation as usury when a good is sold for more than it is worth (*De emptione*); for trade taken in its general sense, it may relate to the determination of the criteria for the licitness of the exchange given by the triptych person, time, mode (*In IV Sent.*, d. 16, q. 4, a. 2, qc. 3), and of the licitness of the expenses reflected in the price (*De emptione*, III); finally, in limit cases, the analytical error may relate to the nature of the exchange ratio to which the exchanged good belongs (*Super Isaiam*, 55, 1) and to the nature of the qualitative constraints reducing the possibilities of sales (*In IV Sent.*, d. 36, q. 1, a. 2).

The qualitative risk also comes into play when *the criteria of justice are implemented*, once they have been determined. In the case of monetary loans, since the principle is that of equality between the sum lent and the sum returned, and since Aquinas does not consider exchange or inflation, but rather a nominal value, there is no risk of error in the implementation. The compensation provided for in later works by extrinsic titles (*damnum emergens* in *S. T.*, IIa IIae, q. 78, a. 2, ad 1 and the *poena conventionalis* in *De malo*, q. 13, a. 4, ad 14) is not, however, specified as to how it is to be calculated, which gives rise to a risk of error and injustice when it is applied. In the case of forward sales, how is the value of what the property is worth on the common market determined, and does the method of estimation lead to a reliable approximation (*De emptione*)? In the general case of the activity of merchants, do the person and the day correspond to the criteria (error on the status of the person or on the calendar of non-working days), and is there no error in the understanding of the fraud or in the licitness of the contract (*In IV Sent.*, d. 16, q. 4, a. 2, qc. 3)? When applying the exchange ratio in limit cases, are the various variables correctly evaluated and weighted?

Thus, before venturing any analysis and external contribution based on the Thomasian works, these writings already provide an initial typology of risk. Any subsequent elaborations must therefore be based on these elements, provided by Aquinas himself, and must always be related to them as a check on their conformity with the sources they comment on.

Three Types of Risks: Analysis Risk, Commercial Risk, Strategic Risk

A new typology emerges from a reading of Aquinas's early works, based on the first explicit classifications that are combined in them. Although it is not yet a broad elaboration, and while keeping to a strict reading of the text, we can break down risk into three types according to its internal or external origin. Some are caused by the co-contractor, whose intention remains hidden and who can benefit from an asymmetry of information—this is the strategic risk; others, finally, are caused by events external to the exchange and its agents—this is the commercial risk. We could relate analytical risk to commercial risk, since it is caused by the moralist, whose erroneous judgement weighs externally on the agents of the exchange. However, the characteristics of this risk lead us to treat it in a specific way (Table 3.2).

The *risk of analysis*, which is a risk of misunderstanding the activity, is the first risk highlighted by Aquinas. This is a peculiarity arising from the type of discussion aimed at a just moral appreciation and that is made possible by the framework offered by the scholastic *disputatio*, where the arguments are discussed. However, his contribution in this respect has applications that go beyond the context of the thirteenth century, since it states the possibility of poor judgement on the part of the expert and implicitly suggests the consequences. This is an indirect risk: it arises from the moralist's poor analysis, but it is incurred by the agents more than by the moralist himself. It is a risk to one's moral and legal reputation, for example of being wrongly considered as a usurer (*In III Sent.*, d. 37, a. 6; *De emptione*); or as a merchant who does not sell at the right price, either usuriously or by including illicit expenses in the price, that is, made imprudently (*De emptione*); or as a merchant who does not respect the qualitative conditions established for trade in general, for example, selling on feast days, or with fraud or not according to a licit contract (*In IV Sent.*, d. 16, q. 4, a. 2, qc. 3); or who does not respect a particular good's trading rule, for example, that the married serf cannot be sold far away (*In IV Sent.*, d. 36, q. 1, a. 2); or who sells a good according to a wrong exchange ratio, for example, a cleric asking a fee (price) for mass (*Super Isaiam*, 55, 1; *In IV Sent.*, d. 25, q. 3, a. 1, qc. 1; Januard and Lapidus 2023, 126–130; Januard 2025a). This risk of analysis is also quantitative, since agents may find themselves unjustly deprived

Table 3.2 Types and levels of risks in the *Commentary on the Sentences*

Type *Level*	*Analysis risk (1)*	*Commercial risk (2)*	*Strategic risk (3)*
Licitness	Subjective risk of misunderstanding trading Reduction of the risk of lack of information on the intention by considering a systematic illicit trading RTcs1–2; RTcs6; RTcs12	Reduction of the risk of non-supply of the city by prohibiting trading RTcs3	Increased strategic risk to the customer due to lack of information about the merchant's intention and circumvention of merchant's status RTcs11
Conditions	Risk of misunderstanding of the conditions of justice of the means of trade RTcs4–5; RTcs9; RTcs10	Shifting the risks arising from the merchant's bargaining power by applying conditions. Reduction of the customer's commercial risk. Increase in the merchant's commercial risk, which leads to a supply risk for the city RTcs3; RTcs8	Risk of circumvention of trading conditions by the merchant due to the imprecision of the mode "without fraud and according to a licit contract" RTcs11
Remuneration	Risk of conceptual imprecision of remuneration RTcs7	Risk that the merchant's remuneration is too low, leading to a supply risk for the city RTcs3	Risk of information about the merchant's intention using the conceptual imprecision of remuneration RTcs3

of an activity that is nevertheless licit, or may be harmed by a price whose justice is erroneous (since the process of estimating the just price involves an approximation), or may be harmed in their remuneration if an error affects its nature or amount. This is the case with merchants, where the clause "without fraud and according to a licit contract" (*In IV Sent.*, d. 16, q. 4, a. 2, qc. 3) requires further clarification by Aquinas, which he provides in the *Summa theologiae* using the traditional Roman *duplus* rule to frame the price so that it can be just if it is between half and twice the purchasing price (*S. T.*, IIa IIae, q. 77, a. 1, ad 1).

The content of the other risks is more familiar to economic analysis. *Commercial risk* is the risk that arises in the course of the transaction and is not due to the behaviour of the co-contractor. This is typically the risk of price fluctuations over time. It is implied on two occasions in *De emptione*: on the one hand, when Aquinas considers that usury occurs when a good is sold for more than it is worth "on the common market [*secundum communem forum*]" (*De emptione*, II), since the price found on the market varies; and on the other hand, when merchants, by imprudent spending, increase their risk of loss (*De emptione*, III), since for Aquinas the prudent person is one who foresees (*porro videns*) and who "sees the happenings of uncertain things [*incertorum videre casus*]" (*S. T.*, IIa IIae, q. 47, a. 1, resp.; Januard 2022b, 253–251; Januard 2024a, 430–432). The commercial risk also affects the lord if he cannot find a way to sell his married serf at the right price on the spot, as he does not have the right to sell him far away so as not to undermine his marriage. Finally, as the loan is presented as a commercial exchange in which the sum returned is equal to the sum lent (*In III Sent.*, d. 37, a. 6), the analytical framework for the risk of a loan is that of a commercial exchange. The risk of this commercial exchange is still zero, since the practice of charging interest is prohibited. There is therefore as yet no risk on the amount of the interest, that is, on the price of the exchange, since this price is not yet free to fluctuate. Furthermore, Aquinas does not foresee any default in payment. However, a risk of a commercial nature gradually appears with extrinsic titles, since Aquinas allows *damnum emergens* (*S. T.*, IIa IIae, q. 78, a. 2, ad 1) and *poena conventionalis* (*De malo*, q. 13, a. 4, ad 14). These titles introduce a financial compensation to the lender. Agents are therefore faced with a risk regarding the common evolution of the terms of these titles.

Strategic risk arises from the agent's ignorance of the motivations and future actions of the co-contractor. The risk may arise from the usurious intention of the lender who conceals the interest behind extrinsic titles (*S. T.*, IIa IIae, q. 78, a. 2, ad 1) or forward sales (*De emptione*). It may also result from the intention to include illicit expenses in the price (*De emptione*, III). It also arises from the seller's intention not to respect the licit conditions of his activity: to be a merchant while he is a cleric or monk, on a prohibited day or with fraud, under an illicit contract or without respecting the contract (*In IV Sent.*, d. 16, q. 4, a. 2, qc. 3). This risk also arises from the intention not to respect the criteria of justice of the exchange, such as the geographical criterion that forbids selling the married serf far away (*In IV Sent.*, d. 36, q. 1, a. 2), or from the intention to sell a good which cannot be the subject of a price or which must be exchanged for a specific counterpart, for example, a spiritual good (*Super Isaiam*, 55, 1; *In IV Sent.*, d. 25, q. 3, a. 1, qc. 1). Strategic risk comes from the unknown intention of the co-contractor. Aquinas pursues a goal of moral discernment aimed at determining whether the agent is committing a sin, which depends on his intention. However, since intention remains hidden, Aquinas circumvents the lack of information about this intention by looking for objective and visible indicators of the justice of the exchange. He therefore focuses his interest on the price and the good exchanged. This reduces the strategic risk, since the agent circumvents his ignorance of his co-contractor's intention by ensuring the justice of the exchange through these two indicators within his reach.

This general typology can be cross-referenced with specific typologies that emerge from a reading of Aquinas's texts. This is the case with the activity of merchants in the *Commentary on the Sentences*, whose licitness is a licitness of means: the person and the day must be appropriate, and the activity must be carried out without fraud and according to a licit contract (*In IV Sent.*, d. 16, q. 4, a. 2, qc. 3). This brings out three levels at which a risk appears: the licitness of commercial activity, the conditions under which this activity is carried out, and the remuneration of this activity. In fact, by focusing on the means in his response without repeating the prohibition which appears in the *sed contra* and which he inherits from Peter Lombard and Gratian, Aquinas leaves the licitness of commerce in a form of methodological *epoché*. There therefore remained a risk as to the legality of the activity itself, since it was not until the *Summa theologiae* (*S. T.*, IIa IIae, q. 77, a. 4, resp.) that the liceity of trade was established both on the basis of its means (moderate gain) and its end (helping the poor, supporting one's family, supplying the country). Secondly, the conditions under which the trade is carried out are also subject to risk: while the persons and days on which the trade is licit are well known, the concepts of fraud and the licitness of the contract are less precise. Finally, the risk may appear at the level of the remuneration of the commercial activity, since this is limited upwards by the need for the absence of fraud and compliance with the contract, but not downwards by protection of the seller, since only fraud by the seller is envisaged. We can cross-reference these three levels of risk (licitness, conditions, remuneration) with the three types of risk (analysis risk, commercial risk, strategic risk), since each of the three types can be found at each level (Januard 2022c).

This gives us a set of nine commercial risks:

Licitness is the first level of risk incurred by the merchant. It involves three types of risk. First, there is *a risk of analysis and understanding* (1), since by not having access to the intention of the transaction, observers cannot fully understand the trade and therefore treat it according to their subjective situation, and, as a result, by conceptual approximation, either assimilate this lack of information to a systematically bad purpose, as Gregory VII and Peter Lombard do, which leads to a complete condemnation of the transaction, or provisionally confine themselves, as Aquinas does, to a moral determination concerning the means of the transaction. This risk of understanding thus results in a legal and moral reputation risk for the merchant, since it calls into question the very licitness of their activity. The risk of legality is also *a commercial risk* (2) for the whole city, namely one of supply, from which Aquinas maintains a certain distance but which remains present not only in his first writings on trade (*In IV Sent.*, d. 16, q. 4, a. 2, qc. 3, obj. 1; *De regno*, II, 7 (II, 3)) but also late in the *Summa theologiae* (*S. T.*, IIa IIae, q. 77, a. 4). Finally, there is *a strategic risk* (3) for the client, because the merchant's intention and the aim of his activity remain hidden and the merchant can, in order to sustain his activity by evading questions about its licitness, circumvent his status as a merchant.

The conditions for the practice of the activity of trade (the prohibition on clerics, the limitation to certain specific days, the requirement to practice without fraud and according to a licit contract) allow Aquinas to outline a double criterion of justice, both quantitative and qualitative. This attention to the means, through conditions which, in particular for the absence of fraud, are somewhat imprecise, creates a *risk of analysis* (1) which is a risk of misunderstanding the conditions of justice relating to the means of trade. There is also a *commercial risk* (2) because the conditions are not there to favour the practice but represent a constraint that limits the activity: in addition to the fact that part of the population is excluded from the activity, merchants cannot sell on certain days, a licit contract represents a formal constraint of an administrative nature, and the absence of fraud entails both qualitative and quantitative constraints (limitation of the price upwards). The conditions reduce the customer's commercial risk in the face of the merchant's bargaining power, but they also impose a commercial risk on the merchants and thus a supply risk on the population. Finally, there is a *strategic risk* (3), since the conditions imposed on the practice of trade enable Aquinas to reduce the strategic risk arising from the hidden nature of the merchant's final intention, but open up the possibility for the latter to take advantage of the imprecision of these conditions and to envisage ways of circumventing them.

The merchant's remuneration also encounters three types of risk: a *risk of analysis and understanding* (1) arising from the conceptual imprecision of the requirement of the absence of fraud and compliance with a licit contract in order to establish the conditions of remuneration. A *commercial risk* (2) which takes the form of a price risk for the merchant, since the condition of a "fraud-free" transaction and the compliance with "a licit contract" is disadvantageously asymmetrical for him. This gives rise to a supply risk for the population, if the remuneration risk results in the merchants' activity being halted. Finally, there is a *strategic risk* (3) for the customer, as the merchant's possible intention to take advantage of the conceptual imprecision of his income and the imprecision of the level of the demarcation remains hidden.

Building a Broad Hermeneutic of Thomasian Risk

While economic analysis provides an initial understanding of the texts on lending and trade, a global and distanced reading of Aquinas's work offers an additional hermeneutical stage. On the one hand, it mobilises the conceptual apparatus Aquinas employs in philosophy and theology. This reading is particularly fruitful for taking a new step towards understanding the central economic concept of the just price in Thomasian thought. It is also a question of discerning not only the explicit or implicit nature of risk but also the role Aquinas plays in its emergence. His analysis, through its emphases and choices, gives rise to new risks.

An Analytical Elaboration of a Three-Level Just Price and Related Risks

The first analytical typology consists of decomposing the central concept of Thomasian economic thought, namely the just price, in order to highlight the nature of the risks involved at each stage, drawing on the entire corpus and conceptual apparatus of Aquinas. We are therefore engaging here in a hermeneutical act which, unlike previous typologies, no longer stops at the letter of the text but seeks to perceive its implicit underpinnings.

Analogy and Sign

The gradual rediscovery of the primacy of justice in understanding the just price, and of the distinction between the price of justice, according to a justice that pre-exists exchange, and effective just prices, belonging to a set of acceptable prices (Lapidus 1994), opens the way to a new stage. The first typology is based on an understanding of the just price based on two conceptual instruments used by Aquinas in philosophy and theology: *analogy* and the *sign*. Aquinas does not explicitly formulate this approach to price, but it is consistent with his philosophical apparatus and with what he says about the just price in his various writings (Januard 2022d, 755–764).

The first instrument of analysis is *analogy*. Aquinas uses the concept in his theory of language to deal with divine names (*S. T.*, Ia, q. 13, a. 5 and 6, see Chollet 1903, col. 1142–1154; Montagnes [1963] 2008; Gilson 1965, 121–129; Te Velde 2006, 109–121; Imbach and Oliva 2009, 83–84; Bonino 2016). Analogy makes it possible to avoid an *equivocity* according to which names as applied to God and as applied to created realities would take on different meanings, to the point where man would have no access to the meaning of a word as applied to God and could say nothing about Him; and to avoid a *univocity* that would reduce this meaning to that known to men, which would undermine divine transcendence. The analogy of proportionality constitutes a middle way where what is said is right, but the reality described exceeds what is said. This link of resemblance between the first reality (God) and the second reality (the created reality) is made possible by the relationship of creation. There is therefore neither dissimilarity nor identity between the primary reality and the reality that derives from it. Aquinas himself applies this analogical link between justice and the just price in the *Commentary on the Sentences* when he deals with simony through the use of the expressions "*sicut cum*" and "*cum*" (as):

> If it is with respect to quantity [*in quantum*], then there is injustice [*injustitia*], as [*sicut cum*] when someone does not buy or sell at a just price [*non justo pretio*]; but if it is with respect to the object [*in quid*], as [*cum*] when he sells or buys what is not the object of a price [*quid non cadit sub pretio*], then it is the sin of the simoniac. (*In IV Sent.*, d. 25, q. 3, a. 1, qc. 1, resp.)

Sicut cum and cum take on an analogical meaning. The sale and the price are given here as examples and belong to the situations of injustice described by the general framework of the proposition, but they do not express the entirety of what the injustice is and are only an actual and visible manifestation of it. The occurrences of these expressions in the *Commentary on the Sentences*, and more generally across all of Aquinas's works, attest to these three dimensions of an analogical expression: a known manifestation that describes a primary term that is directly inaccessible and that lies upstream, where what is said by the example is true, but the example does not say everything. The use of *sicut* and cum, through the polysemy of the terms and their comparative meaning, introduces a distance (Quicherat 1893, 279 and 1035; Blaise 1954, 233–234 and 758; Ernout and Meillet 2001, 156, 561 and 756–757). There would not be a strict identification between justice and just price, not because the just price would not be just, which would be a contradiction in terms, but because the registers of justice and of the effective just price of the exchange in question here would not be superimposable. Moreover, in *In IV Sent.*, d. 25, q. 3, a. 1, qc. 1, it is not strictly speaking price and justice that are related to each other, but justice and an action that occurs. This is underlined by the temporal value of cum and *sicut* cum. Moreover, *sicut* always introduces a comparison that relates to the quality of the thing (Gardin-Dumesnil 1845, 295 and 352), here the sale. The injustice is thus about the transaction and not about the price itself.

Aquinas also introduces an analogical treatment of the just price through the expression "*secundum*" used in *De emptione*: the price is not just if goods are sold for more than they are worth "on the common market [*secundum communem forum*]" (*De emptione*, II), an expression already found in Albert the Great: "according to the estimate on the market [*secundum aestimationem fori*]" (Albert the Great, *In IV Sent.*, d. 16, a. 46). The preposition *secundum* introduces both a linkage and a distancing between the two terms. In *De emptione*, II, *secundum* actually links three terms: the price of the singular good ("they sell the cloth for more [*plus vendant pannos quam*]"); the value on the common market, that is, the common value of the good ("than what they are worth on the common market [*quam valeant secundem communem forum*]"), whether or not the act of sale on that market takes place; and the price on the market when the sale takes place, since the value must be translated into a price so that the price of the particular sale can be compared to it. *Secundum* here introduces a ratio, but not an equality, between these three terms.

Indeed, *secundum* primarily means "behind", then "along with", then, in a temporal meaning, "immediately after"; this then gives it the meaning "second", "of a lower rank". These meanings lead to a fourth meaning, "according to", "in accordance with", "in favour of" (Quicherat 1893, 1013; Ernout and Meillet 2001, 608). In the Middle Ages, the preposition takes on a temporal, causal and final meaning: "at the moment of", "as a result of", "in view of" (Blaise 1975, 833), "during", "following", "regarding", "for", "in the aim of" (Blaise 1954, 747). The sense of conformity is broadened both quantitatively and qualitatively, to include the locative: "in proportion to", "in the same manner as", "in" and "among" (in the Hellenistic sense); and a distributive sense: "simultaneously", "at the same time". Depending on the meaning chosen for *secundum*, the link between the three terms may be different: if we choose a simple locative or temporal meaning, the value of the good, its price on the market and its singular price can proceed in parallel without interacting, as something situated along the edge of a sea (*secundum mare*). If we envisage a meaning in the sense of a "manner" or "means", the singular just price should conform to the value of the good, translated by the market into the price, in the way that an agent might conform to the law (*secundum legem*).

The only occurrence of a variant of "*secundum communem forum*", is in *In III Sent.*, d. 37, a. 6, and the four occurrences of *forum* in the sense of market (*In I Sent.*, d. 37, q. 3, a. 2, ad 3; *De malo*, q. 1, a. 3, ad 16; two in *In Physicorum*, l. 2, n°2 and n°7) are temporal and locative, the last three occurrences being found in the expression "going to the market". There are also 395 occurrences of the form *foris*, often in the general Latin locative sense of "to be outside", "in the square" or "at the market". It would therefore seem that it is difficult to consider the market as an immaterial principle which would determine a singular material reality which would be value. It is more likely that the market is, on the contrary, the place of value's manifestation.

However, in Aquinas's works, *secundum* as a preposition is used in a way that might suggest, if not a causal sense, then at least a sense of subordination, when the referent (in the accusative case) is a principle that has ontological precedence over the subject, which is a concrete reality, as is the case in expressions such as "*secundum rationem* [according to reason]", "*secundum esse* [according to being]", "*secundum justitiam* [according to justice]", "*secundum legem* [according to law]" or "*secundum veritatem* [according to truth]". The general principle constitutes the reference to which the subject conforms. Here, the manifestation of value enables a comparison to be made between actual prices, on the market on the one hand, and in the singular sale by the merchant on the other hand. For the comparison to be possible, the meaning to be retained is undoubtedly also that of conformity, and not just that of a simple temporal or geographical conjunction. But the market is only an intermediary level here, the place where the justice of the price is manifested, a manifestation which, through conformity, makes possible a singular exchange that is just. However, this link of conformity prevents us from considering an identity between value, market price and singular price. We thus see, through the analogical lexicon used by Aquinas, an application of the just price to three levels of reality: it is the price of justice, but also by analogy the effective just price on the market, and again by analogy, the just price in the singular exchange.

The second instrument, which Aquinas does not refer to in relation to the price but which forms part of the general framework of his analysis, is the philosophy of the *sign*, which he uses in theology to deal with the sacraments and which enables him to describe three levels of reality of a sacrament (e.g. *In IV Sent.*, d. 3, q. 1, a. 1, qc. 1, ad 1 and *S. T.*, IIIa, q. 73, ad 3; see Michel 1939; Revel 2004; Rosier-Catach 2004). The typical case is that of the sacrament of the Eucharist: the bread and wine are the sign of a sacred reality, the body and blood of Christ, which they become by transubstantiation during the Mass. This sacred reality, although the sacrament is fully achieved, is itself the sign of an ultimate reality, the grace conferred on those who receive them. In the same way, although there is no question here of superimposing situations, we can envisage three levels of reality for the just price. In *De emptione*, the singular price is just if it conforms to the price charged on the common market (*secundum communem forum*). But the expression *secundum* on the one hand and the notion of estimation on the other hand refer to a pre-existing reference. The formulations used in *De emptione* therefore indicate that the fairness of this price on the market is placed in reference to a prior justice to which it refers. The just price can thus take three different levels.

Three Levels of Reality

The just price in the singular exchange would be the sign (*sacramentum tantum*, sign only) of the just price on the market (*sacramentum et res*, sign and thing), which itself would be the sign of the ultimate and hidden reality (*res tantum*, thing only) that would be the price of justice, that is, the price according to the justice which pre-exists the exchange, which is not visible and directly accessible but is manifested by the effective prices charged on the market and in the singular exchange. The comparison needs to be adapted, since, in Aquinas's sacramental theology, the sacrament is already fully realised in the *sacramentum et res*, at the second level, whereas the price of justice, to which acceptable prices refer, is at the third level, but it is interesting to see how the expression "just price" can be understood at different levels of reality. In addition, we can see that in the case of the price, as in the case of the sacraments, these three-level sets are divided into two: the first two levels for the accomplishment of the sacrament, then one level for its effects; two levels of effective price and one level of just price as the price of justice.

We can add to this reading of the just price according to three economic levels of reality a reading according to three legal levels of reality. Aquinas considers that merchants must operate "without fraud and according to a licit contract [*secundum licitum contractum*]" (*In IV Sent.*, d. 16, q. 4, a. 2, qc. 3, resp.). The use of the preposition "*secundum*" here again marks the ratio of conformity and not of identity between the three levels of exercise of the right, just as it indicated conformity without identity in economic terms in *De emptione* through the expression "according to the common market [*secundum communem forum*]" (*De emptione*, II). The exchange must be carried out according to the singular contract, which must conform to the positive law of contracts, which determines its licitness. This positive law must itself conform to natural law, which pre-exists it.

Indeed, for Aquinas, positive law is simply the application of the normative moral justice that precedes it and that is expressed in a universe of acceptable positive rights: "The human will can, by virtue of a common convention [*ex communi condicto*], make something just among those things that of themselves imply no opposition to natural justice. And it is here that there is room for positive law" (*S. T.*, IIa IIae, q. 57, a. 2, ad 2). The justice that pre-exists exchange thus manifests itself economically in the market price and then in the singular price, and legally in contract law and then in the singular contract.

The just price, which is the price of justice, is found, by analogy and as a sign, in the just price on the market, and also, by analogy and as a sign, in the just price of the singular exchange. Each of these three levels can give rise to each of the three types of risk (analysis risk, commercial risk, strategic risk).

This gives us a set of nine fundamental risks affecting the just price (Table 3.3):

The risk of analysis and understanding occurs as a risk of error concerning the nature and criteria of justice of the just price (first level of reality of

Table 3.3 Types of risks according to the levels of reality of the just price in *De emptione*

Risks *Price*	*Analysis risk*	*Commercial risk*	*Strategic risk*
First level of reality Normative just price	*First level of analysis risk* Risk on the criteria of justice: • Lack of precision of *De emptione* on the criteria of justice. Lack of information, moral and legal RUde1–2; RUde4	*First level of commercial risk* Risk of plurality of acceptable prices: • Just price but not the most advantageous price for the agent within the set of acceptable prices RUde3	*First level of strategic risk* Circumvention of the notion of justice or interpretation for usurious purposes by the contracting party: • Lack of information on the intention of the contracting party and on the true criteria of justice RUde1–2
Second level of reality Price on the market	*Second level of analysis risk* Risk of error or approximation: • When estimating in order to translate the just price into price on the market RUde3; RUde5–6	*Second level of commercial risk* Risk of market price fluctuation: • In time and space RUde3–4	*Second level of strategic risk* Risk of price manipulation strategies: • The contracting party passes off as a non-usurious price on the market a price that in reality includes time RUde1–4
Third level of reality Price in the exchange	*Third level of analysis risk* Risk of error on the value of the good and on the acceptable elements in the price: • Lack of precision of *De emptione* on the definition of value, on the concept of usury and on the content of the acceptable effective price RUde4	*Third level of commercial risk* Risk of bargaining power: • Unfavourable situation, within the set of acceptable prices, due to the conditioned will or necessity to carry out the exchange in a time and place in which the market price is unfavourable RUde4	*Third level of strategic risk* Individual usurious risk: • Usurious strategic behaviour of the contracting party accepted out of necessity (conditioned will) or by lack of information RUde1–2

the just price). There is a moral and legal risk for all agents, buyers and sellers alike, who may all find themselves in a situation of usury. It also occurs as a risk of error and of approximation concerning the effective just price on the market, which is based on an estimate (second level of reality), and as a risk of error about the value of the individual good and the content of the acceptable effective price, and on what it can incorporate (third level of reality).

The commercial risk occurs as a risk of a plurality of acceptable prices that are consistent with the normative just price (first level of reality), a risk of a fluctuating price on the market (second level of reality), and a risk concerning bargaining power, as the agent may be in an unfavourable situation due to his conditioned will (third level of reality).

The strategic risk occurs as a strategic risk of the co-contractor circumventing or interpreting notions of justice and usury for usurious purposes (first level of reality), a strategic risk of price manipulation by passing off the usurious price as the non-usurious price on the market (second level of reality) and an individual strategic usurious risk (third level of reality). Indeed, the intention of the contracting party to deliberately take advantage of the conditioned will, universalised in *De emptione*, or of the agent's particular lack of information, remains private information and is hidden.

Three Extensions of Risk: Explicit Risks, Implicit Risks, Induced Risks

Risk can also be read according to another typology, which has to do with its formal expression or extension. This typology can only be brought to light by a hermeneutical act. This, then, is no longer a question of giving an account of Aquinas's thought, but of analysing the levels of discourse at which risks are situated: some risks are *explicit*, some are *implicit*, and some are *induced* by Aquinas himself, his understanding of economic activity giving rise to these risks.

Explicit Risks

Indeed, certain risks are *explicit* in the early works, notably through the lexicon chosen by Aquinas related to *probability*, *prudence* and *danger* (Januard 2024a).

The lexicon of *probability* is introduced by the expression "*satis probabilis* [rather probable]" (*In III Sent.*, d. 37, a. 6) in the *Commentary on the Sentences*, Aquinas's first text of economic significance. In this great early work he evaluated the arguments of the authorities against usury and pronounced on the traditional view of lending as a *mutuum*, a transfer of property. A set of elements relating both to *In III Sent.*, d. 37, a. 6, to Aquinas's use of the term *probabilis*, and to the notion of probability before the advent of the calculus of probabilities five centuries later, leads us to consider here the expression of a doubt. There is a risk about the correctness of the understanding of the operation, which is probable and not certain. The lack of certainty concerning the justification of the prohibition of usury entails risks for the moral and legal reputation of the lender and has repercussions on all related activities and their agents: borrowers, buyers and sellers forward (*De emptione*), as well as the prince and the population according to the use that can be made of the taxes levied on usurious gains (*Ad ducissam Brabantiae*).

In addition, Aquinas introduced the notion of the "*aestimatio*", which is understood as an approximation that is made when agents try to find the just price on the market (*De emptione*, I; *S. T.*, IIa IIae, q. 77, a. 1, ad 1). Thus, there is not only a qualitative risk of analysis but also a quantitative risk of calculation. The innovative character of Aquinas's approach can be highlighted here, as he mentions, in these early writings, the risk of error in the analysis and in the calculation, which would in a sense correspond today to the risk of error on the part of the economist, who may misunderstand economic mechanisms or miscalculate. Economic activity is a world of people making decisions, acting upon them, and sometimes making mistakes: the moralist or the economist can be wrong when analysing operations as well as agents. Although they are honest and want to exchange at the just price, they can make mistakes. To get around the impossibility of knowing the agent's intention, which remains hidden, Aquinas develops an objective analysis of the transaction and its justice by focusing on the visible conditions of the exchange, such as the price, rather than on the subjective intention of the agents. However, the human dimension of economic activity, complete with its risk of error, remains.

This human aspect leads to another manifestation of probability: one must add the notion of fraud (*fraus* and *fraudulentia*), not so much as regards the secrecy of its intentionality as for its objective consequences. Over the course of his life, we can see an evolution in the vocabulary Aquinas uses. In the *Summa theologiae* in general, and *S. T.*, IIa IIae, q. 77 in particular, he uses *fraudulentia* and its derivatives, which appear twice in the question, alongside *fraus* and its derivatives, which appear six times. Whereas *fraus* (fraud) is a more legal term (Langholm 1992, 223) that characterises an action, *fraudulentia* (deceit, malice, the work of one who does wrong) is more characteristic of the person who carries out this action (Blaise 1954, 364; Blaise 1975, 401; Bréal and Bailly 1918, 105; Ernout and Meillet 2001, 252), with, on the one hand, the idea of being filled with fraud, and to live with fraud like a habit (Gardin-Dumesnil 1788, 301), and, on the other hand, a closeness to theft, since fraud involves using deception to take something that belongs to someone else (Barrault and Grégoire 1853, 634). These two characteristics of *fraudulentia*, habit and proximity to theft, appear in *S. T.*, IIa IIae, q. 56, a. 2, ad 3. The context is a response concerning vice (*actum vitii*), mentioned in objection 3, and vice is a bad *habitus*, and therefore has a repetitive dimension; moreover, Aquinas enumerates the three places in which cunning is executed (*ad executionem astutiae*), namely theft (*furto*), calumny (*calumnia*) and fraudulent sale (*fraudulenta venditione*), thus showing the proximity of these three actions. The introduction to *S. T.*, IIa IIae, q. 77, "on the deceit [*de fraudulentia*] which is committed in purchases and sales [*quae committitur in emptionibus et venditionibus*]", thus marks a double evolution in relation to the *Commentary on the Sentences*: there is an extension of his account to encompass the purchasers, whereas *In IV Sent.*, d. 16, q. 4, a. 2, qc. 3 is limited to the sellers; there is a semantic reinforcement of the moral dimension of the analysis. Two instruments then allow Aquinas to reduce the lack of information about the justice of the exchange. First, the consideration of all agents, and second, the idea of the repetition of injustice, contained in the structural dimension underlined by *fraudulentia*. He does not, then, revert to a subjective moral reading but rather deepens the reduction of the risk of analysis by seeking visible and objective criteria of injustice, in this case recidivism. The morality and intention of the agent, which remained hidden, thus become observable.

Commercial fraud does not constitute an archetypal expression of risk, but its possibility involves a risk. Indeed, there is a possibility that the co-contractor could behave in a manner contrary to justice and that this could result in damage to the agent. Fraud is first mentioned in the *Commentary on the Sentences* in relation to professional commercial activity (*In IV Sent.*, d. 16, q. 4, a. 2, qc. 3), before being discussed in a more general way in the *Summa theologiae* in relation to any exchange activity and to any buyer or seller (*S. T.*, IIa IIae, q. 77).

The lexicon of *prudence* appears in the *De emptione*. Aquinas distinguished between expenses that the merchant may licitly include in the price and those that he may not. These illicit expenses are incurred when a merchant borrows to develop his business and, more generally, they refer to the expenses of the merchant made imprudently, namely "*incaute* [without precaution]", and "*imprudenter* [unwisely]" (*De emptione*, III). Aquinas thus differentiated between two stages within the exercise of prudence: namely an absence of negligence and, then, good management. Although Thomasian prudence is a virtue, which is not an object of calculation (Yuengert 2012, 57, 74–75; Hirschfeld 2018, 179), it can be compared with the contemporary understanding of prudence as an aversion to an increase in the risk of loss (Kimball 1990; Januard 2022b). Thomasian imprudence affects both trade and lending, since it is manifested in purchases made with a view to sale, although the ultimate imprudent expenditure is the taking out of a loan.

The lexicon of *danger* first appears through the term *discrimen*, which can mean "critical point of danger" as employed in the more economic part of *De regno*, Aquinas's political treatise that lies between his early and later works. Aquinas uses the term in the phrase "various dangers of the ways [*diversa viarum discrimina*]" in the context of a consideration of the transport risks incurred by merchants (*De regno*, II, 7 (II, 3)). The economic questions of the *Summa theologiae*, for their part, mention danger four times in the form of the term *periculum* (danger). The first is the risk of transport, which can justify an increase in price (*S. T.*, IIa IIae, q. 77, a. 4, ad 2), thus affecting seller and buyer. Then there is the risk incurred by the buyer of a dangerous good (*S. T.*, IIa IIae, q. 77, a. 3, resp. and ad 3) and the resulting constraints on the seller. Finally, the notion of danger is essential to the Thomasian understanding of economic activity since it serves to distinguish between the loan as *mutuum*, which is a transfer of property where the lender does not incur any risk and therefore cannot claim any gain, and the model of *societas*, which is more akin to an acquisition of a shareholding (*S. T.*, IIa IIae, q. 78, a. 2, ad 5). Moreover, *De malo* puts the treatment of danger into perspective by placing it in the moral framework of the exercise of the virtues, since one cannot sin or incite to sin in order to avoid a danger, but a poor person can borrow out of necessity by taking advantage of the malice of one who is already a usurer (*De malo*, q. 13, a. 4, ad 19).

Implicit Risks

Although there are a few formal expressions of risk, the presence of this risk is most often *implicit* and emerges from the situation described. For instance, in the first directly economic text, Aquinas reviews the three arguments of the authorities against usury. None of them is fully satisfactory or self-sufficient. There is therefore a risk of misunderstanding what interest-bearing loans are. This risk is certainly explicit concerning the *mutuum* argument, judged *satis probabilis*, but it is more widely implicit. Aquinas proposes three arguments and not just one, and he keeps the sources anonymous and general: "everybody says in a general way that giving with a view to usury is a mortal sin. But different reasons are given. Some say ..." (*In III Sent.*, d. 37, a. 6). Aquinas thus implicitly suggests a certain weakness in the arguments and the need to combine them, which he does in subsequent writings by combining the argument pertaining to the *mutuum* and that pertaining to the nature of money.

Similarly, in *De emptione*, the situation of a seller who transfers a good at a future date for more than it is worth on the market, or of a client who imposes a discount for early payment, appears to be a situation that could arise. In addition, by listing the expenses that may or may not be licitly included in the price, Aquinas implicitly suggests that this list may not be obvious to everyone, or that transgressions may occur on the part of sellers. Moreover, we can see that they are trying to legitimise the inclusion of loan expenses in the sale price by means of an argument that Aquinas contests.

It is therefore likely that some are trying to include them in an effective way. In the same way, setting out the conditions for the activity of merchants (*In IV Sent.*, d. 16, q. 4, a. 2, qc. 3) or for the sale of a married serf implies that it is possible that they will not be respected. The risk remains of trade being carried out by a cleric or a monk or on a feast day, or with fraud and without licit contract. In the same way, the lord can try to sell his married serf in remote regions, even if it is prohibited.

Furthermore, there is a risk on the nature of the exchange ratio. Specifying that certain goods cannot be exchanged according to a price implies that the risk of this happening is not zero, to the extent indeed that such an act can be given a specific name, such as simony (*Super Isaiam*, 55, 1; *In IV Sent.*, d. 25, q. 3, a. 1, qc. 1). Conversely, *Super Isaiam*, 55, 1 shows that there is a risk that a man will not pay the just counterpart, to the point where the situation was understood until the beginning of the thirteenth century as a gift rather than an exchange.

Finally, the attention devoted to the *quid*, to the nature of the object exchanged, brought to light through the treatment of simony, suggests that there may be an error in the identification of this *quid* and in the understanding of the exchange ratios that it commands. There is therefore a risk of attributing a wrong exchange ratio to the good, for example, according to the example given by Aquinas, by attributing a price to something that cannot have one, but which can be exchanged rather in the stipend mode (*In IV Sent.*, d. 25, q. 3, a. 1, qc. 1).

Induced Risks

A third degree of extension of risk also appears in Aquinas. Now, it is no longer a question of explicit or implicit risk, but of the *induced risk* that can arise from the Thomasian analysis, not so much because of an error in the analysis as because of its orientation. The first example is the risk induced by the expression "without fraud" which applies to the merchant (*In IV Sent.*, d. 16, q. 4, a. 2, qc. 3). On the one hand, the concept still needs to be specified quantitatively, which Aquinas will do in the *Summa theologiae* with the *duplus* rule that frames the allowed price (*S. T.*, IIa IIae, q. 77, a. 1, ad 1). On the other hand, Aquinas is only concerned here with one of the co-contracting parties, and the merchant is the only one who has constraints imposed on the exercise of the transaction. No conditions are imposed on the buyer. The attention paid to merchants, a new and rapidly developing social group whose activities are unknown and also suspect because of the risk of usury or fraud, and who have strong bargaining power, entails a risk for their remuneration, which is only limited upwards, and a risk for the justice of the exchange arising from abusive behaviour on the part of the buyer, which is ignored here. *De emptione* proposes a more balanced and symmetrical view, with the possibility that the buyer may find himself in the position of a usurer if he demands a discount for early payment. The *Summa theologiae* reinforces this symmetrical view, with the seller also being able to contravene the justice of the price (*S. T.*, IIa IIae, q. 77, a. 3, resp.).

The other example is the risk of supply. The *Commentary on the Sentences* states in objection 1 that "[The community] cannot be preserved without [...] trade, by which the people procure the necessities of life" (*In IV Sent.*, d. 16, q. 4, a. 2, qc. 3, obj. 1), but Aquinas does not take it up again, nor any reason for legitimising trade, in the *respondeo* of this sub-question. *De regno* is more nuanced, because the city can live either from its local production or from trade, and "it is demonstrated that the first means is the most advantageous [*convenientior esse manifeste convincitur*]" (*De regno*, II, 7 (II, 3)). Supply is necessary, but when local production is not enough, and we have to resort to trade, this is the cause of many harmful social consequences (Januard 2022c, 66; Januard 2024b,

507, 525–526), although it fosters international friendship (Santori 2019, 81–87; Santori 2021, 18–19). Indeed, trade involves many risks: a risk of dignity, since a thing is more dignified (*dignius est*) if it is sufficient for itself, and it is more dignified for a territory not to depend on another; a risk of supply, since economic independence is safer (*securius*) for supplies, "because of wars and risks of transport [*diversa viarum discrimina*]"; a risk of cultural corruption, because trade involves contact with foreigners, whose company most often corrupts (*extraneorum conversatio corrumpit*) the morals of citizens; a risk of moral corruption because "if the citizens themselves indulge in trade [*si cives ipsi mercationibus fuerint dediti*], the door will be open to many vices", everything in the city will become venal (*ut in civitate omnia fant venalia*), which will thus be laid open to fraud (*locus fraudibus apertitur*); a military risk with the weakening of the army if the soldiers commit themselves to trade, whose characteristics soften the soul and make the body debilitated; and a political and public order risk, since trade encourages gatherings, which are conducive to sedition.

In the *Summa theologiae*, trade allows that "the things necessary [*res necessariae*] for the life of the country are not lacking [*ad vitam patriae desint*]" (*S. T.*, IIa IIae, q. 77, a. 4, resp.), but this trade must be for a "moderate gain", a strong constraint that shows that supply is not an absolute priority and remains subordinated to the justice of the exchange. Moreover, in *Ethicorum*, V, 9, Aquinas differs from his authorities (Langholm 1984, 32) by not noting, contrary to Aristotle (*Nicomachean Ethics*, V, 5, 1133a) and especially to Albert the Great in his two commentaries on Aristotle's *Ethics* (*Ethicorum*, written in 1250–1252, ed. Cologne, V, VII, 403–404 and V, IX, 413 (see Kübel 1968–1972, VI); and *Ethicorum*, written after 1260, ed. Borgnet, V, II, 9), that the cessation of exchange resulting from the absence of a just price (Hollander 1965, 619–621) will affect all crafts and lead to the fall of the city (Hamouda and Price 1997, 195). Whereas this social consequence is developed at length in Albert's two *Ethicorum*, it is absent in Aquinas.

It is clear that Aquinas is aware of the need for merchants' activity in society. However, if we observe the distance he takes from the expression of this necessity, in parallel with his insistence on the limitation of income, we can consider that a risk arises from his analysis, as this limitation could lead to a halt in activity and a shortage in the city.

Setting out the conditions for the activity of merchants (*In IV Sent.*, d. 16, q. 4, a. 2, qc. 3) or for the sale of a married serf also implies induced risks. The risk of trade being carried out involuntarily by a cleric or a monk or on a feast day is low, but the concept of the absence of fraud and the licitness of the contract remains sufficiently imprecise that a risk of confusion, even unintentional, is possible, as the role of *duplus* remains implicit in Aquinas's works until the *Summa theologiae* (*S. T.*, IIa IIae, q. 77, a. 1, ad 1). Lastly, the geographical clause prohibiting the distant sale of the married serf may on the one hand be transgressed and on the other hand be misinterpreted, as the notion of "remote areas" is not strictly defined (*In IV Sent.*, d. 36, q. 1, a. 2, ad 4).

Another induced risk may be highlighted by the way Aquinas addresses the sinful nature of merchants. To establish that merchants are often, but not always, in a sinful situation, Albert relies on the biblical verse Ecclesiasticus 26:28, which mentions two moral difficulties for those who trade: negligence for the merchant and the sin of the tongue for the innkeeper (*caupo*, which also means a petty tradesman or a huckster): "It is difficult for the merchant to avoid negligence, and the innkeeper will not be justified for his sins of the tongue [*peccatis labiorum*]" (Albert, *In IV Sent.*, d. 16, a. 46, s. c.). The practice of the profession without sin is therefore difficult, but not impossible. Aquinas did not use this quotation in his own *Commentary on the Sentences*, but he did use it again 15 years later in the *Summa theologiae* to justify the prohibition on clerics trading: "it is difficult for a merchant to avoid sins of the tongue [*difficiliter exuitur negotiator a peccatis labiorum*]" (*S. T.*, IIa IIae, q. 77, a. 4, ad 3). Aquinas truncates the quotation by omitting the innkeepers and negligence: the sin of the tongue, peculiar to the innkeeper, is now attributed to the merchant (Januard 2023, 648). Neglect, which remains in Albert's quotation, was dealt with by Aquinas in 1262, ten years before the *Summa theologiae*, in *De emptione*, III, through the adverb *incaute* (without attention) attributed to the merchant. Here, however, only the sin of the tongue affects the merchant. It could be argued that the sin of the tongue is a commercial one. In Roman law, some contracts, such as *stipulatio*, are oral (*verbis obligatio*). Sales rather belong to the consensual contracts (*consensu obligationes*), which are not explicitly oral, but which may be achieved without scriptures (*sine scriptura*) (Justinian, *Institutiones*, III, 15 and 22–23). In this way, Aquinas may be thinking of a more or less oral bargaining. It could also be argued that this sin is not directly commercial but is rather linked to the restlessness of the merchant's life, which coincides with the second sin mentioned: "trade greatly monopolises the mind through attention to secular things [*negotiatio nimis implicat animum saecularibus curis*]", which "distracts from spiritual things [*spiritualibus retrahit*]" (*S. T.*, IIa IIae, q. 77, a. 4, ad 3). Is Aquinas's shortcut the result of an economic understanding, is it the result of a deliberate attempt to redirect thinking about the nature of merchants' sin to their social life rather than to their commercial practice, or is it the result of a quick summary of his master's thought on a subject that is not at the heart of his thinking? The sin of the tongue seems more relevant to the innkeeper than to the merchant, although it can indeed be one of his sins. The consequence for understanding the risk of moral condemnation hanging over the profession is, however, a major one: is it the professional practice itself, or simply the social conditions of the activity, that are a source of sin?

A final induced risk needs to be mentioned. Aquinas's texts dealing with economic issues provide scattered elements which, if combined, would make it possible to reconstitute a set of typologies, as we have just done, or even a kind of global explanatory model, as we shall do in the next section. However, Aquinas does not express this directly. There therefore remains a risk of error in understanding Aquinas's works. The debates on usury and the just price that have agitated commentators throughout the twentieth century show that no interpretation can be considered as self-evident and definitive. The risk of error is certainly reduced by the principle of non-contradiction, that is, the fact of verifying the compatibility of any attempt at conceptualisation with all the relevant texts. There is therefore little risk of proposing totally erroneous interpretations. However, there is still a risk of departing from Aquinas's way of thinking.

A Dynamic Approach to Risks

Mapping and then classifying and combining the emerging risks in Aquinas's work provides the basis for an analytical approach, not only with a view to producing static typologies but also a dynamic representation of the structure of risk. Economic activity unfolds in successive stages and through many stakeholders. The most obvious case is that of forward sales, where buyer and seller can adapt their behaviour between sale and settlement, but this is more generally the case for any commercial activity, since the merchant buys, transports and resells. The dynamic character of economic activity can also be identified in another aspect, where time is not broken down into days but into stages of analysis with a view to carrying out a transaction in accordance with justice. Even in the case of an instantaneous transaction, certain stages are involved upstream and downstream of the transaction. Risks therefore come into play at these different stages, both upstream and during the transaction.

A Panoptical and Intertemporal Economic Approach

There is an evolution in the way Aquinas deals with situations of commercial exchange or loan in the course of his works. At first, the focus is mainly on the lender and the seller, before being extended to the borrower and the buyer. In his quest for justice in the transaction, Aquinas naturally focused his attention on the agents most likely to engage in unjust practices because of their greater bargaining power and better information: merchants and usurers. However, he quickly moved away from this social view of certain types of agent, considering that the buyer could also find himself in a sinful situation. He adds to this a dynamic vision of the exchange by considering how it unfolds over time, since the situation of the agents can change in the course of the transaction. This extension leads to a form of panopticon where the exchange is observed in its entirety in space and time, not only from the point of view of each of the co-contractors but also from the point of view of the implications of the exchange for the population as a whole. This leads to a global view of the risk, incurred by all stakeholders and at all stages of the activity.

Sellers were identified with the professional merchants who travelled the roads of Europe from fair to fair. These merchants of various sizes formed a new social category with growing power. They were well versed in contracts (including written ones), account books (or books of reason more broadly), accounting, foreign exchange, navigation and commercial law. The scope of their activities was not yet clearly defined, which could lead to suspicions of usury (Spicq 1935, 392–399; McLaughlin 1939, 1940; De Roover 1953, 28–29; Le Goff [1956] 2001, 9–67; [2010] 2019, 121–231; Dupuy 1992, 25–59; Dellemotte 2017, 25; Ege 2014, 392; Feller 2020, 57–61). The usurers, for their part, were still seen at the beginning of the thirteenth century as exploiting the poor, who borrowed out of necessity. Although there were already analyses of the nature of lending, such as Robert of Courçon's *De usura*, the condemnation of usury was still largely social rather than economic. In 1140, Gratian still equated lending at interest with murder (Gratian, *Decretum*, II, causa 14, q. 4, c. 11) and William of Auxerre, in the first half of the thirteenth century, considered that "usury is directly against charity" (William of

Auxerre, *Summa aurea*, III, XLVIII, c. 1, q. 1, l. 5). The non-professional co-contractor, that is, the buyer or borrower, is therefore at a disadvantage, either because he is in a state of necessity, or because he has less knowledge of the state of the market and current prices on the one hand, or of his rights on the other hand. From text to text, however, Aquinas progressively distances himself from these presuppositions, gradually coming to observe all the parties involved in the exchange.

Although the early writings seem to focus more on the activities of the lender and the seller and are therefore more asymmetrical in their treatment of the agents than the later writings, we must immediately point out a major original exception. Indeed, the treatment of the situation described in the first text in which Aquinas evokes the "just price", namely his commentary on Isaiah 55:1, written several years before his first directly economic texts, the articles on merchants and usury in the *Commentary on the Sentences*, can be seen as heralding the future developments in Thomasian thought (Januard 2025a). This text already introduces a broader perspective. Indeed, the biblical passage seems to focus entirely on the buyers: "All you who are thirsty, come to the waters" (Isaiah 55:1). The seller's activity remains unspoken, and there is mention only of a purchase and buyers. This is perhaps explained by the particular identity of the seller, namely God, who is also the one who speaks through the voice of the prophet. Aquinas, on the contrary, begins by mentioning the seller, in this case God, who has made a promise: "Then [God] makes a promise, promising future abundance to those in need: 'all you who are thirsty'" (*Super Isaiam*, 55, 1). The specific conditions of the sale, which are then presented to the buyers, are the ways in which the divine promise is fulfilled: they can make a purchase without money and for the right price. All the parties involved in the transaction are therefore taken into account by Aquinas. It should be noted here, however, that this attention to the seller is not motivated by a moral examination of his behaviour, as in the case of earthly commerce, but shows that God initiates the sale and sets the conditions.

Having made this initial exception, we can see that the early writings are relatively one-sided. This can be seen in the two directly economic articles of the *Commentary on the Sentences*. In the first, which deals with the situation of usury in the lender, Aquinas does not dwell on his sinful intention, but on what the loan consists of, which because of the nature of money and of the loan conceived as a transfer of property where the risk is borne by the borrower cannot be the object of interest. Furthermore, almost the entire article deals with the action of lending and not that of borrowing. Only the final response to the objections, that is, the last lines of the article, turns to the side of the borrower, who is not in a sinful situation if he is in a state of necessity (*In III Sent.*, d. 37, a. 6). The second, which deals with commerce, takes the same unilateral approach. The text deals with the activity of merchants, without mentioning the buyer (*In IV Sent.*, d. 16, q. 4, a. 2, qc. 3). Aquinas specifies the conditions for the licitness of this activity: trading cannot be licitly carried out by clerics and monks, who may however sell their own goods; it must take place at the set time, not on feast days; and must be according to the due mode, that is, without fraud and according to a licit contract. The buyer appears only allusively in the first objection, which justifies trade on the basis of the need for supplies. Indeed, commerce is "that by which necessary things are procured for the people". Only the reference to the people (*populo*) evokes the final non-professional customer.

The two texts in the *Commentary on the Sentences* that refer to the "just price" mark an initial opening up to all the parties involved, although they remain more focused on the seller. Firstly, simony is presented as an act of buying or selling: the simoniac "buys or sells what cannot be priced" (*In IV Sent.*, d. 25, q. 3, a. 1, qc. 1, resp.). However, the purchase in question here is not so much the final purchase of the person who wishes to use sacred powers illicitly as the purchase of the person who trades in them by reselling them. Thus, Simon the Magician, who wanted to buy these powers from the apostles (Acts of the Apostles 8:9–24) and who gives his name to this sin, is considered by Aquinas to have wanted to buy the power in order to resell it (*In IV Sent.*, d. 25, q. 3, a. 1, qc. 1, ad 4). Aquinas's attention is therefore still focused on the activity of the merchant, even though he is presented here as the buyer.

Then, when Aquinas deals with the sale of a married serf, he presents the situation from the point of view of the lord, in this case the seller, in order to determine the conditions of the sale, and of the serf, in this case the property sold (in the economic sense, although he is a person), in order to recall his freedom to marry without his lord's authorisation and the need for the lord not to interfere with this marriage by a distant sale (*In IV Sent.*, d. 36, q. 1, a. 2). We are therefore talking here about the seller and the property he is selling but not the buyer.

Around five years later (1262), *De emptione* marks the first major step towards a global vision of exchange in space and time. The title refers to a twofold operation: buying (*de emptione*) and selling (*et venditione*). In

Roman and Canon law, buying and selling constitute a unique operation (Justinian, *Institutiones*, 3, 23; Gregory IX, *Decretales*, l. 3, t. 17). Aquinas keeps the phrase "*de emptione et venditione*" as describing a unique operation, but he breaks down the transaction to specify what is the seller's and what is the buyer's concern. The text focuses on the activities of merchants, but Aquinas describes a situation in which the buyer plays as active a role as the seller. In fact, the merchant who sells his goods at a future date above the just price "because of the expectation [*propter expectationem*]" is in a situation of usury, but this is also the case of the buyer, who is in a usurious situation by obtaining a discount for early payment that leads to a price lower than the just price:

> This is why, in the proposed case, there would be more reason to fear being a usurer for the buyer who, by paying before three months, pays less for cloth than the just price, than for the seller who receives less for being paid earlier. (*De emptione*, I)

The possibility of a sinful situation thus affects all agents, but to this extension in space must be added an extension in time, since it is during the transaction that the buyer asks for a discount and places himself in the position of a usurer.

It should be noted, however, that the context is that of the mediaeval Champagne fairs, where merchants gather and meet from all over Europe. *De emptione* describes the activities of the Tuscan merchants who come to sell their cloth at the Lagny fair. The buyer was therefore not a private individual but another professional, who also had good information and obviously possessed strong negotiating power, and who bought to resell. As in the case of simony, the purchase is not made by a final consumer but by a professional reseller, whose activity Aquinas seeks to identify as possibly sinful.

This broadening of perspective is also evident when he discusses the case of the merchant who borrows to develop his business (*De emptione*, III). Here, the merchant is seen as a borrower who commits a sin since he contributes to usury even though he is not forced to do so by necessity, unlike the particular borrower who borrows out of necessity in the *Commentary on the Sentences* (*In III Sent.*, d. 37, a. 6). Aquinas also refers to the imprudent spending of merchants, "*incaute et imprudenter*". Aquinas implicitly presents the merchant as a buyer through the loan that provides him with the necessary initial capital outlay, and through his expenditure.

When discussing trade in *De regno*, a few years later (c. 1265–1267), he still focuses on merchants. However, Aquinas's view of the consequences of mercantile activity for society is broader and more ambivalent than in the *Commentary on the Sentences*. While this activity makes it possible to obtain supplies, it also presents social and cultural risks for the city. It should be noted, however, that the broader perspective here focuses more on the consequences of trade for the city than on the situation of the various parties involved in the transaction, since it only refers to the foreign sellers who bring their goods, or the citizens who would be encouraged to imitate them, but not directly to the customers.

In the *Letter to the Duchess of Brabant* (1271), which deals with what the prince can do with the taxes levied on usurious gains, Aquinas opens his view to the other parties involved and to the subsequent transactions, since he studies the consequences of usury for the prince and for the transactions he may carry out with the tax levied on usury. There is thus a broadening of the social viewpoint, close to that of *De regno*. Three aspects of this letter indicate a universalisation and objectivity of approach. Firstly, although the question from Margaret of Constantinople, Countess of Flanders, concerned the Jews, whom she equated with usurers, Aquinas responded with an objective judgement on the activity practised, regardless of who practised it: "the Jews, or some other usurer", and by explaining: "What we have said about the Jews also applies to the people of Cahors [a city with a reputation for high levels of usurious activity] and to all those who indulge in the vice of usury". Aquinas then extends his analysis, as is traditional, to the borrowers, who are victims of usury, since it is to them that the tax levied must be returned first and foremost. Finally, Aquinas extends his view to the population as a whole, moving from restitution within the framework of commutative justice to distributive justice, since the money must be devoted to "pious uses, according to the advice of the diocesan bishop and other wise men, or for the common good of the country, if necessity threatens or the common good so requires" (*Ad ducissam Brabantiae*).

The major development occurs in the *secunda secundae* of the *Summa theologiae* (1272), where Aquinas extends his analysis to commercial activity in general, which is assumed to be good since it is practised "in the interests of the parties" (*S. T.*, IIa IIae, q. 77, a. 1, resp.). Trade "for gain [*propter lucrum*]", the professional activity of merchants, which is opposed to natural exchange for the household, is only a special case, occurring in the last of the four articles of q. 77, on commercial fraud. While in the early works economic activities were treated in dispersed order, Aquinas unites them here under the heading of voluntary exchange (Januard 2022a), which groups together commercial exchange and lending (*S. T.*, IIa IIae, q. 77, prol.). The social and professional status of the agents, as merchant or usurer, as well as their intention, is no longer the common grid for analysing exchange. With a few specified exceptions, such as in the case of exchange for gain, exchange is viewed bilaterally, as both a purchase and a sale, without regard to the person involved.

With the *Summa theologiae*, bargaining power and the benefit of better information shift from one agent to another. Sellers are no longer just professional merchants with a high level of knowledge and power. This can put the buyer in a dominant position. This is particularly the case if the seller of a property with a defect communicates this defect when it is visible and the price has already been legitimately reduced. Aquinas advises the seller not to disclose information unless the defect represents a danger, as the buyer could take advantage of this to demand an exaggerated discount (*S. T.*, IIa IIae, q. 77, a. 3, resp. and *II Quodl.*, q. 5, a. 2, resp.). To ensure the justice of the exchange, Aquinas must therefore make sure that all the agents act justly, since each of them might not do so.

We are thus witnessing a gradual universalisation of Aquinas's view, in both space and time. He emancipates himself from the presupposed power of the agents (a professional merchant seller, a usurious lender who exploits the poor who borrow out of necessity) and their sinful intentions, and considers that in the course of the exchange, each of the co-contracting parties may be guilty of usury or charge an unjust price. This leads him to adopt an overall view of the exchange that is accompanied by a concomitant increase in the number of explicitly named risks, implicit risks that appear through the situations described and the agents evoked, and induced risks, since through each of the questions he leaves unanswered or the imprecision of his lexicon, Aquinas introduces new risks.

A Three-Stage Dynamic Approach to Risk

The risks presented in the various early writings of Thomas Aquinas can be assembled to highlight their internal dynamics. There are two levels at which risk may come into play: before the exchange and during the exchange. There is then a descending and ascending progression, which can be represented in the form of a diagram that bears some parallels to the plan of the *Summa theologiae*, known as *exitus-reditus*, exit-return

(Aquinas starts from God, deals with creation and humanity, and then shows how man, through Christ and the sacraments, can return to God). In the early works, we see two fundamental risks, in the primary sense of the term: a fundamental risk for economic analysis, in the sense that it lies at the foundation of the analysis of the operation, since it affects this analysis itself; and a fundamental risk for the economic operation, which affects the foundation of the justice of exchange, since it concerns the exchangeable character of the good. This risk, which is the first in the order of nature, since it concerns the nature of the good before any exchange and any analysis of exchange, is nevertheless the last in the order of knowledge. If it pre-exists exchange, it is only revealed by the application of the criteria of justice of this exchange, namely a quantitative criterion (level of the exchange ratio, such as the price) and a set of qualitative criteria, which will be reduced to the *quid*, the nature of the good. Risk can therefore be represented in the following dynamic structure (Fig. 3.1):

An upstream risk. The first expression referring to risk is used by Aquinas in his first writing of a directly economic nature, *In III Sent.*, d. 37, a. 6. Presenting the arguments of the authorities against usury, none of these arguments seems to fully satisfy him. The first argument, monetary, seemed insufficient, "which is why others give another reason". Aquinas then presents the traditional conception of lending as a *mutuum*, a transfer of property, which implies the absence of interest. This argument is presented as *satis probabilis*, rather probable (*In III Sent.*, d. 37, a.

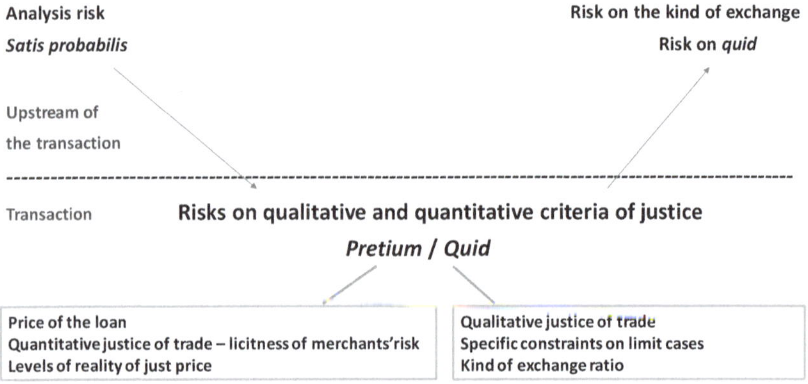

Fig. 3.1 Representation of the dynamic structure of risk in early works of Thomas Aquinas

6, resp.). The first risk exposed by Aquinas is therefore not a risk incurred during the transaction but a risk of error in analysing and understanding the transaction. The concepts used to analyse the transaction may be erroneous: the question of the fungibility of money has not yet been resolved with certainty for Aquinas in the *Commentary on the Sentences*, and the understanding of the loan as a *mutuum* remains probable but not certain. The risk therefore appears upstream of the economic activity, since an error of understanding of the transaction entails a multiple risk for the agents: risk of moral and legal reputation; financial risk, since the licit exchange, which is made in the interests of the parties (*S. T.*, IIa IIae, q. 77, a. 1, resp.), cannot be carried out because it is considered illicit; risk for the merchant of not being able to pass on in the price an expense deemed imprudent (*De emptione*, III); but also risk for external stakeholders, such as the prince, who cannot do as he pleases with the taxes collected on a gain considered illicit, in this case the proceeds of usury, but who must return them to the persons supposedly harmed (*Ad ducissam Brabantiae*).

Risks in the operation. Then there are the risks that arise in the course of the transaction. Since the fairness of the exchange depends on both qualitative criteria (non-financial conditions) and quantitative criteria (price), the risk of unfairness may affect both sets of criteria. The loan may be subject to a consideration that is not fair, with the presence of interest, which would mean that the sum returned is not equal to the sum lent (quantitative criterion). It can also be subject to unjust extrinsic titles, not in terms of amount but of nature (qualitative criterion), for example, a *lucrum cessans* (*S. T.*, IIa IIae, q. 78, a. 2, ad 1). Similarly, commercial activity must be carried out "without fraud and in accordance with a licit contract" (*In IV Sent.*, d. 16, q. 4, a. 2, qc. 3, resp.). Fraud and the contract have a quantitative dimension, which affects the price, and a qualitative dimension (deception regarding the goods or the wording of the contract).

Forward sales, described in *De emptione*, also present a qualitative and a quantitative risk. There is a risk in terms of price, since there is usury if the cloth is sold for "more than it is worth" (*De emptione*, II). Similarly, in the case of forward sales, Aquinas states in *De emptione* that the activity of merchants is limited by what they can or cannot include in the price, that is, licit or illicit expenses. The risk is ultimately a quantitative risk, since the risk of injustice in the exchange is a risk that weighs on the fair price, and the risk incurred by the merchant is that his expenses will be deemed illicit and that he will not be able to recover them in the sale price. However, the distinction that leads to these price risks is both qualitative and quantitative. Aquinas regards a merchant's borrowing to develop his business and imprudent expenditure, either through negligence (*incaute*) or poor anticipation (*imprudenter*), as illicit expenditure. The notion of prudence used here is similar to that found in contemporary literature (Kimball 1990), where it refers to an increase in the risk of loss. The imprudence may be qualitative, if the merchant buys goods at a price that is too high or buys too much, wrongly anticipating the quantities and the selling price. However, imprudence is also, and undoubtedly primarily, qualitative. There are two arguments in favour of this qualitative criterion: on the one hand, the first illicit expenditure is qualified by its nature, a loan to buy goods; on the other hand, considering the nature of the expenditure is consistent with the attention to the object (*quid*), which governs the possibility and conditions of sale in *In IV Sent.*, d. 25, q. 3, a. 1, qc. 1 and in *In IV Sent.*, d. 36, q. 1, a. 2, instead of the qualitative criterion ensuring the justice of the exchange in *In IV Sent.*, d. 16, q. 4, a. 2, qc. 3.

We can thus see the emergence of a risk which, in the course of the transaction, may affect the qualitative and quantitative dimensions of the exchange, which can be reduced to two criteria, the price and the thing exchanged. The first occurrences of the expression "just price" confirm, through limit cases, that these two criteria are indeed, on the one hand, those that ensure the justice of the exchange and, on the other hand, those that bear the risk of the transaction.

From his first use of the expression "just price", Aquinas envisages that certain exchanges take place according to an exchange ratio that is not a price, since there are situations where, in order to be just, the exchange would have to be at an unjust price, which is not possible. This is the case of the exchange between God and man in *Super Isaiam*, 55, 1, and then in later works the case of the income of the lawyer, the doctor, the merchant, the soldier, the lender who issues extrinsic titles, or the priest. Exchange does not take place on the basis of a price, in the sense of an equality of thing to thing, but the conceptual tool of price makes it possible to think of these transactions within the framework of exchange and not within the framework of gift. The existence of this plurality of exchange ratios makes it possible to think of all these transactions, but entails a risk of error as to the nature of the right exchange ratios. What appears in this first instance of the expression "just price" continues in the next two. It is the nature of the object exchanged, the *quid*, that will determine the nature of the exchange and the criteria taken into account in the exchange ratio. The notion of exchange and the notion of price and fair price are therefore introduced through limit cases that restrict commercial exchange: the sacrament, which cannot be sold, in *In IV Sent.*, d. 25, q. 3, a. 1, qc. 1; or the married serf, who cannot be sold away without damaging his marriage, in *In IV Sent.*, d. 36, q. 1, a. 2.

The *quid* can act as a qualitative element of justice within the commercial exchange and implies a risk of injustice during this exchange. This is the case, for example, in the situation in which the third occurrence of the expression "just price" occurs: the married serf can be sold at a just price (quantitative criterion), but a non-financial (qualitative) criterion is added to establish the justice of the exchange, in this case the geographical criterion.

Back to upstream risk. However, the *quid* may also determine the very nature of the exchange and its possibility (Januard 2023, 2025b). It implies a risk of error as to that nature and the risk of carrying out an exchange that can only be unjust if it does not conform to the nature of the property exchanged. This risk lies upstream of the exchange, since it relates to its possibility and nature, not to the way in which it takes place. It appears in the first occurrence of the expression "just price" (an exchange between God, who gives his grace, and the human being, who provides a limited counterpart, taking into account his resources) and continues in the second (the sacrament cannot be sold, but the priest can be paid a subsistence allowance on the occasion of the sacrament). This risk concerning the *quid* is chronologically the first to appear in the early writings, *Super Isaiam* predating the *Commentary on the Sentences*. It can thus be noted that the two risks located upstream of the transaction, the risk on the quid and the risk of analysis, are chronologically (at least if we assume that the *Commentary on the Sentences* was written in the order of the text) the first two: *Super Isaiam*, 55, 1 and *In III Sent.*, d. 37, a. 6. However, these two risks are each located at one end of the risk chain and act as a framework for the transaction risks. The risk of analysis is visible before the exchange and is formulated by Aquinas, if not explicitly, then at least straightforwardly (e.g. with the expression "*satis probabilis*"), not in the context of a concrete case of usury but in a review of the argumentation, which is situated upstream of any usurious transaction. The risk on the *quid*, although already present, only appears on the occasion of the actual exchange, and Aquinas only formulates or implies it within the very description of the exchange (exchange between God and man and simony, unjust sale of the sacrament).

A dynamic structure of risks can therefore be derived from the early writings, ranging from a fundamental risk (analysis) to another fundamental risk (*quid*), via the risks on the two criteria of justice during the transaction, that is, the quantitative criterion assimilated to price and the qualitative criterion, assimilated to *quid*.

References

Primary Sources

Albert the Great. 1891. *Ethicorum* [second commentary], ed. Borgnet, t. 7. Paris: Vivès.

———. 1893–1894. *In librum sententiarum*, ed. Borgnet, t. 25–30. Paris: Vivès.

———. 1968–1972. *Super Ethica* [first commentary], ed. Albertus-Magnus-Institut (Cologne), t. 14 (1). Aschendorff: Monasterii Westfalorum.

Aristotle. 1903. *Ethica Nicomachea*, editio altera, ed. Franciscus Susemihl and Otto Apelt. Leipzig: Teubner.

———. 1970. *L'Éthique de Nicomaque*, introduction, traduction et commentaire par René Antoine Gauthier et Jean Yves Jolif, I, 2. Louvain: Publications universitaires/Paris: Béatrice-Nauwelaerts.

Bréal, Michel and Bailly, Anatole. 1918. *Dictionnaire étymologique latin*. Paris: Librairie Hachette et Cie. Kimball, Miles S. 1990. Precautionary Saving in the Small and in the Large. Econometrica 58 (1): 53–73.

Corpus Juris Canonici. 1661. Lyon: Laurent Anisson.

Corpus Juris Civilis. 1803. Metz/Paris: Behmer et Mamort/Rondonneau.

Gregory VII. 1853. Concilium Romanum V. In *Patrologiae cursus completus*, series Latina, t. 148. Paris: J.-P. Migne.

Peter Lombard. 1916. *Libri IV sententiarum*, t. 1 and 2. Claras Aquas: Typis Collegii S. Bonaventurae, Quaracchi.

Robert of Courçon. 1902. *De usura*, ed. Georges Lefèvre, Lille: Travaux et mémoires de l'Université de Lille.

Thomas Aquinas. 1884. *Commentaria in octo libros physicorum Aristotelis*, ed. Leonina, t. 2. Rome: Typographia polyglotta S. C. de Propaganda Fide.

———. 1888. *Summa theologiae*, Ia, qq 1–49, ed. Leonina, t. 4. Rome: Typographia polyglotta S. C. de Propaganda Fide.

———. 1897. *Summa theologiae*, IIa IIae, qq. 52–122, ed. Leonina, t. 9. Rome: Typographia polyglotta S. C. de Propaganda Fide.

———. 1906. *Summa theologiae*, IIa IIae, qq. 40–60 sup., ed. Leonina, t. 12. Rome: Typographia polyglotta S. C. de Propaganda Fide.

———. 1929–1947. *Scriptum super Sententiis*, 4 t. Paris: P. Lethielleux.

———. 1969. *Sententia libri Ethicorum*, ed. Leonina, t. 47. Rome: Commissio Leonina.
———. 1974. *Expositio super Isaiam ad litteram*, ed. Leonina, t. 28. Rome: Santa Sabina.
———. 1979. *Opuscula III*, ed. Leonina, t. 42. Rome: Commission Leonina.
———. 1982. *Quaestiones disputatae de malo*, ed. Leonina, t. 23. Paris/Rome: Commissio Leonina—J. Vrin.
———. 1996. *Quaestiones de quolibet*, ed. Leonina, t. 25.2. Paris/Rome: Commissio Leonina—ed. du Cerf.
William of Auxerre. 1980–1987. *Summa aurea*. Paris/Grottaferrata: ed. du Centre national de la recherche scientifique/Editiones Collegii S. Bonaventurae ad Claras Aquas.

Secondary References

Barrault, Émile, and Ernest Grégoire. 1853. *Traité des synonymes de la langue latine*. Paris: Librairie Hachette et Cie.
Blaise, Albert. 1954. *Dictionnaire latin-français des auteurs chrétiens*. Strasbourg: ed. Le latin chrétien.
———. 1975. *Lexicon latinitatis Medii Aevi*. Turnhout: Brepols.
Bonino, Serge-Thomas. 2016. *Dieu, "Celui qui est": de Deo ut uno*. Paris: Parole et silence.
Chollet, Arthur. 1903. Analogie. In *Dictionnaire de théologie catholique*, t. 1. Paris: Letouzey et Ané, col. 1142–1154.
De Roover, Raymond. 1953. *L'évolution de la lettre de change*. Paris: Librairie Armand Colin.
Dellemotte, Jean. 2017. *Histoire des idées économiques*. Paris: Dunod.
Dupuy, Claude. 1992. De la monnaie publique à la monnaie privée au bas Moyen Âge (XIIIe et XIVe siècles). *Genèses* 8: 25–59.
Ege, Ragip. 2014. La question de l'interdiction de l'intérêt dans l'histoire européenne. *Revue Économique* 65 (2): 391–419.
Ernout, Alfred, and Antoine Meillet. 2001. *Dictionnaire étymologique de la langue latine*, 4th edition revised. Paris: Klincksieck.
Feller, Laurent. 2020. Les écritures de l'économie au Moyen Âge. *Revue Historique* 693: 25–65.
Gardin-Dumesnil, Jean-Baptiste. 1788. *Synonymes Latins*. Paris: Nyon le jeune.
———. 1845. *Synonymes latins*, revised ed. by Jules-Antoine Auvray. Paris: Jules Delalain.
Gilson, Étienne. 1965. *Le thomisme*, 6th edition revised. Paris: Vrin.
Hamouda, Omar, and Betsey Price. 1997. The Justice of the Just Price. *European Journal of the History of Economic Thought* 4 (2): 191–216.
Hirschfeld, Mary L. 2018. *Aquinas and the Market*. Cambridge: Harvard University Press.

Hollander, Samuel. 1965. On the Interpretation of the Just Price. *Kyklos* 18: 615–634.

Imbach, Ruedi, and Adriano Oliva. 2009. *La philosophie de Thomas d'Aquin*. Paris: Vrin.

Januard, Pierre. 2021. Analysis Risk and Commercial Risk: The First Treatment of Usury in Thomas Aquinas's *Commentary on the Sentences*. *European Journal of the History of Economic Thought* 28 (4): 599–534.

———. 2022a. De l'*œconomia* à l'échange volontaire: la délimitation de l'activité économique chez Thomas d'Aquin. *Revue des Sciences Philosophiques et Théologiques* 106 (4): 567–609.

———. 2022b. Licit and Illicit Risks in Thomas Aquinas's *De emptione et venditione ad tempus*. *Œconomia* 12 (2): 233–271.

———. 2022c. Risks on Trade: The Activity of the Merchant in Thomas Aquinas's *Commentary on the Sentences*. *History of Economic Ideas* XXX (1): 47–98.

———. 2022d. Risky Exchanges: Price and Justice in Thomas Aquinas's *De emptione et venditione ad tempus*. *European Journal of the History of Economic Thought* 29 (4): 729–769.

———. 2023. Chose, activité, agents: Le regard novateur de Thomas d'Aquin sur les opérations économiques. *Revue des Sciences Philosophiques et Théologiques* 107 (4): 641–679.

———. 2024a. Probability, Prudence, Danger: Thomas Aquinas on the Building of the Lexicon of Risk. *Journal of the History of Economic Thought* 46 (3): 421–442.

———. 2024b. Production et échange chez Thomas d'Aquin: L'homme participe-t-il à l'œuvre de création? *Revue des Sciences Philosophiques et Théologiques* 108 (3): 499–533.

———. 2025a. Is God Giving or Trading: Thomas Aquinas's First Use of 'Just Price'. *History of Political Economy*, forthcoming.

———. 2025b. Thomas Aquinas's ontological approach to economic activity. In *Aquinas, Natural Law, and Social Ontology: Historical and Contemporary Perspectives*, ed. Ana Marta González. London: Routledge, forthcoming.

Januard, Pierre, and André Lapidus. 2023. Trading for No Price, Thomas Aquinas on Money Loans, Sacraments and Exchange. In *The Routledge Handbook of Commodification*, ed. Élodie Bertrand and Vida Panitch, 120–133. London: Routledge.

Kübel, Whilelmus. 1968 1972. Prolegomena. In Albert le Grand, *Super Ethica*, ed. Albertus-Magnus-Institut (Cologne), t. 14 (1). Aschendorff: Monasterii Westfalorum, V–XVI.

Langholm, Odd. 1984. *The Aristotelian Analysis of Usury*. Bergen and Oslo: Universitersforlaget AS.

———. 1992. *Economics in the Medieval Schools. Wealth, Exchange, Value, Money and Usury According to the Paris Theological Tradition, 1200–1350* (Studien und Texte zur Geistesgeschichte des Mittelalters, 29). Leiden: Brill.

Lapidus, André. 1994. Norm, Virtue and Information: Individual Behaviour and the Just Price in Thomas Aquinas' *Summa Theologiae*. *European Journal of the History of Economic Thought* 1 (3): 435–473.

Le Goff, Jacques. [1956] 2001. *Marchands et banquiers du Moyen Âge*. Paris: Presses Universitaires de France.

———. [2010] 2019. *Le Moyen Âge et l'argent, essai d'anthropologie historique*. Paris: Perrin.

McLaughlin, Terence P. 1939. The Teaching of the Canonists on Usury (1). *Mediaeval Studies* 1: 81–147.

———. 1940. The Teaching of the Canonists on Usury (2). *Mediaeval Studies* 2: 1–22.

Michel, Albert. 1939. Sacrements. In *Dictionnaire de théologie catholique*, t. 14. Paris: Letouzey et Ané, col. 485–655.

Montagnes, Bernard. [1963] 2008. *La doctrine de l'analogie de l'être d'après saint Thomas d'Aquin*. Paris: Cerf.

Quicherat, Louis. 1893. *Thesaurus poeticus linguae latinae*. Paris: Librairie Hachette et Cie.

Revel, Jean-Philippe. 2004. *Traité des sacrements*, t. 1.1. Paris: Cerf.

Rosier-Catach, Irène. 2004. *La parole efficace*. Paris: Seuil.

Santori, Paolo. 2019. Was Aquinas a 'Universal Economist'? *History of Economics Review* 72 (1): 79–91.

———. 2021. *Thomas Aquinas and the Civil Economy Tradition*. Abingdon/New York: Routledge.

Spicq, Ceslas. 1935. Appendice I: Notes explicatives. In Thomas Aquinas, *Somme Théologique*, Traité de la Justice, t. 3, 257–358. Paris: Éditions de la Revue des Jeunes.

Te Velde, Rudi. 2006. *Aquinas on God*. Aldershot/Burlington: Ashgate.

Yuengert, Andrew M. 2012. *Approximating Prudence*. New York: Palgrave Macmillan.

CHAPTER 4

Concluding Remarks

Abstract Thomas Aquinas did not write a treatise on risk in economics or even on risk in general. He was writing before the theorisation of risk that gradually emerged from the calculation of probabilities in the modern era to the present day. Despite this, the study of Aquinas's treatment of risk has proved fruitful for three reasons: the importance he attaches to economic activity, the period in which he was writing, and the call for a long-term approach to history of economic thought. In addition, Aquinas is often studied for his contribution to economic ethics, but he deserves to be studied from the angle of economic analysis, for his contribution to the understanding of activities and mechanisms.

Keywords Thomas Aquinas • Middle Ages • Risk • Economics • History of economic thought

Thomas Aquinas did not write a treatise on risk in economics, or even on risk in general. He was writing before the theorisation of risk that gradually emerged from the calculation of probabilities in the modern era to the present day. Moreover, while the management of risk, either to protect against it or to take advantage of it, is an explicit feature of contemporary economic activity, in his works it often remains allusive and implicit. Some risks are not even considered by Aquinas, such as the absolute failure to

P. Januard, *Thomas Aquinas on Risk in Economic Activity*,
https://doi.org/10.1007/978-3-031-83825-5_4

repay a debt or the depreciation of a currency, which might lead him to consider a variation in the value of a monetary sum over time. Despite this, the study of Aquinas's treatment of risk has proved fruitful for three reasons:

The first reason is the importance Aquinas attaches in his works to economic activity. Admittedly, this activity attracts his attention only in a few texts, which may seem very brief in relation to the whole of his work, but when these scattered texts are consolidated, the whole proves to be quite imposing and deals with the diversity of all the modalities and stakeholders of economic activity. Hitherto studied in scattered order, at the end of his life, Aquinas would impose a unity on these otherwise isolated works by grouping them in the *Summa theologiae* under the notion of "voluntary exchanges". As long as they were isolated and unrelated activities, the risks associated with each could not be related within a common model. From the moment that commercial exchange and lending become part of a common activity, it is possible to identify a common grid of economic risks. As we have seen, we can then draw up a typology according to these two activities, but also according to the different kinds of economic risks. This leads to a profusion of classifications of risks, depending on their quantitative or qualitative nature (Table 3.1), whether they are analysis, commercial or strategic risks, whether they affect licitness, conditions or remuneration of trade (Table 3.2), whether they constitute explicit, implicit or induced risks, and whether they affect the first, the second or the third level of reality of the just price (Table 3.3).

The second reason lies in the period in which Aquinas was writing, since this was a time of major economic change, with the development of cities, the advent of a new social category—merchants—and the development of large-scale trade. It was also a time when, faced with the de facto development of lending at interest despite its prohibition, the first attempts to legitimise it were made. Aquinas does, however, distance himself from a social perspective in which non-professional buyers and borrowers fall victim to merchants and loan sharks who enjoy strong bargaining power. He observes how the transaction unfolds over time and highlights the risks incurred by each of the agents. Any transaction involves risks for all the agents. The activity that he unifies under the heading of "voluntary exchanges" is therefore an activity that is not occasionally risky depending on the circumstances, but that is intrinsically risky. It is thus easier to see why the first risks relate to understanding the activity and knowing the nature of the object being exchanged. What might have seemed like an attempt to evade and circumvent the agents' intentions, which remain hidden, shapes Aquinas's economic approach. Risk is not primarily the result of a good or bad intention on the part of one agent or another, but of an ignorance that can affect all agents, including spectators, not first on others' behaviour but on transaction itself.

The third concerns the history of economic thought on risk, which needs to be considered from a long-term perspective. Human beings have been buying, selling, lending and borrowing since long before the advent of economic analysis. Although the political and social structure has changed, the fundamental exchange transactions and the risks associated with them have not. Moreover, people were addressing these exchanges and the associated risks long before the advent of an autonomous discipline in modern times. Aquinas marks a milestone in our understanding of economic risk with his precise attention to the details of exchange mechanisms and demonstrates the fruitfulness of the history of economic thought even when this thought is still embedded in philosophy, theology or law. Throughout its history, risk analysis has therefore been profoundly multidisciplinary. Aquinas's contributions are not just descriptions of situations but an already conceptualised analysis of risk. While mathematisation and then economic analysis proper have brought with them refinements that we feel are essential today, the stages that preceded them have not been superseded. On the contrary, they have been given a new status as foundation stones to which we must always return in order to build new elaborations on rock.

The works of Aquinas thus present a conceptual elaboration of risk based on the conjunction between the new social importance of trading and lending activities in his era, the individual writings that Aquinas devoted to these activities, and his conceptualisation of economic activity as a whole. Moreover, while they as yet contain no general conceptualisation of economic activity, the sum of the conceptual elaborations Aquinas develops to account for the different concrete situations he describes forms a kind of puzzle that is striking in its coherence. The diachronic approach, which sets out the development of an author's thought in chronological order over the course of his life, makes it possible to show the internal evolution of Aquinas's work, revealing it to be an exercise of progressive precision and elaboration rather than a series of treatments of different fields of activity. The overview of all the parties involved in the temporal unfolding of the operation, and the attention paid to the conditions of the exchange even before it takes place—even if all presented in a scattered manner—enables it to be reconstituted in the form of a model of a dynamic global representation, which marks a real evolution in relation to the economic writings that precede it.

In order to assess the value of reading Aquinas's work as a basis for contemporary reflection on risk, it is necessary to clarify the relationship maintained by Aquinas between normativity (a given goal, here the search for justice) and positivity (explanation of economic mechanisms). Aquinas's aim is to determine the morality of an activity through the notion of the justice of exchange. The risks highlighted relate, *in fine*, to the justice of the exchange and the morality of the transaction. However, these risks can be broken down into the risks of loss for the agents who would suffer from the injustice of the transaction, or the chances of gain for those who would benefit from it. Although Aquinas's quest is a moral one, the positive analysis he develops in order to rule on the morality of exchange highlights risks that can be read in strictly economic rather than moral terms.

Aquinas is often remembered for his moral preoccupations, and for the contemporary economist, he presents an alien figure, dealing as he did with economic issues at a time when "the market" was still only "the marketplace", and price only a ratio of exchange between one thing and another—not, as it is understood today, the conceptual point of contact between supply and demand. His memory is then summoned with a certain reverence, and with the sense that we approach him on a dual mission: on the one hand, to strengthen the moral standing of the economist who seeks to intervene in economic life in pursuit of a Good whose nature is, nevertheless, delivered from outside economics, or in other words normatively; and on the other words, to act as historians who search the corridors of time for the memories of nascent ideas contained in a literature which is certainly well preserved, but whose language, philosophical presuppositions and style are deeply obscure to us. These two missions, the nobility and interest of which will not be disputed, are nevertheless far removed from simply uncovering the analysis of economic operations and mechanisms that we are entitled to expect from an economist describing risk.

Paradoxically, while economists have turned philosophers or historians in the hope of extracting the quintessence of Aquinas's work, that work has been waiting nearly eight hundred years to be read by economists, *qua* economists, whose primary interest is neither the moral intention of the author nor the period in which he wrote, and whose reverence is only that due to a scientist for what he has contributed to science. Those economist-philosophers and economist-historians who have read Aquinas have indeed made great strides forward, and we are fortunate to be able to stand like dwarfs upon their giant shoulders, as Bernard of Chartres put it in the twelfth century. However, the time seems ripe for us, as economists, and without ignoring morality and history, to read his works simply for their contribution to economic analysis. These works, as they come into focus, may then seem entirely new, just as the *Super Isaiam*, the *Commentary on the Sentences*, *De emptione* and later works have appeared to us here. These works, like all economic contributions past and present, help us to understand what human beings do at all times and in all places: engaging in voluntary exchanges, hoping for a gain and fearing a loss—in short, taking risks.

Afterword

Reading Thomas Aquinas (When an Economist)

One of the qualities of Pierre Januard's book is to enjoin us to read Thomas Aquinas (i.e. an author from the second half of the thirteenth century) with the same objectives in mind as when we read more recent authors like Smith, Marx, Walras or Keynes. Yet it is far from self-evident how one should engage in such an exercise, because of two obstacles of different types. The first relates to the level of the researcher's investigation, and the second to the disciplinary borders of the field in which it takes place.

Questions concerning the level of investigation indeed arise when we are confronted with such immense figures, whose work and life inspire a dedication that goes beyond the analytical effort we have to make to reconstruct, interpret or extend what we discover in their writings. As a result, we are led to focus increasingly on what they intended to do, at the expense of what they actually did. Or, to borrow a well-known distinction from Quentin Skinner (1969), we are led to focus on *what an author meant*—that is, what he wanted to say to his reader—rather than on *what is meant* by what he wrote—that is, on what a fair-minded and sufficiently informed reader ought to understand from his writings. At times, this can prove fruitful, especially in the case of recent authors, for whom we have all the means required to recognise what they intended to do and what

P. Januard, *Thomas Aquinas on Risk in Economic Activity*,
https://doi.org/10.1007/978-3-031-83825-5

they actually achieved. In 1937, for example, Paul Samuelson, who in 1970 was to receive the Nobel Prize in economics, published a short article in which he provided a theory of decision-making over time, known as discounted utility, for which he is universally praised: *this was meant* by the 1937 paper. But was it also *what he meant*? Presumably not. We know that what he meant was related to the possibility of finding a procedure for measuring cardinal utility (see Fiévet 2022)—as indeed he did, in the very same paper.

With Thomas Aquinas, when we try to read his work as economists, things are more complex. We have every reason to be interested in *what he meant* when he wrote on economic issues; and here we have some clues, through, for instance, his references to authorities, or the very nature of the text he was writing. But by following this path, it is difficult to do better than rediscover a few moral precepts with which we were already familiar, and which leave the economist wanting more. So, what if we focus on *what is meant* by what he wrote? This is what Pierre Januard does, typically, for example, when he takes Thomas's early writings, both the non-economic and the (at least partly) economic, seriously enough to draw up a typology of risks according to the economic activity involved (risk on usury, risk on trade and risk on exchange ratio). When Thomas Aquinas was writing about the *Book of Isaiah*, Peter Lombard's *Book of Sentences*, or even about forward buying and selling, it may be that he did not have anything like a typology of risks explicitly in mind and that his priorities were quite elsewhere. We simply do not know. But now that these texts have been written, it would be doing him justice to recognise that *what is meant* by them is a systematic approach to risks according to their object.

The second obstacle that Pierre Januard overcomes in his book concerns the boundaries of his discipline, economics. It is now a commonplace to assert that the kind of crystallisation of economic knowledge that took place towards the end of the eighteenth century had the effect that the answer to an economic question, and all the steps in between, had also to be economic. For example, if we ask today why lending money is rewarded, the answer will invoke the theory of decision in time, particularly the intuitive assumption according to which an agent always prefers to have a good sooner rather than later (the so-called impatience axiom; see Fishburn and Rubinstein 1982). The answer may be supplemented by a reference to the nature and functions of the good lent (money), to the institutions that make its existence possible, and to the need for a positive industrial profit in an economy where most loans are financing production. At no point does such an answer stray from economic considerations. But what if we go back to earlier writers? We know that at the beginning of the nineteenth century, for example, it would have been necessary to take into account demographic arguments, which are now considered to be outside economic knowledge: in two centuries, the boundaries of economics have shifted.

And what if, following Pierre Januard, we go all the way back to Thomas Aquinas? The issue of borders must now be stated differently: no longer are we confronted with borders that may have shifted, but rather with a situation in which even the mere existence of borders surrounding economic statements appears meaningless. We have of course no reason to believe that Thomas, even in his apparently most economic texts—such as the two questions, in the *Summa theologiae*, on buying and selling and on loans—expressly confined himself at every stage of his analysis to the economic dimension of the issues he was discussing. These questions were concerned with sin, an issue which, as economists, we are not particularly well equipped to address, and on which we defer to theology, philosophy, morality or law. Yet Pierre Januard guides us across these disciplinary boundaries with rare skill; and above all, as his readers will notice, he never lets them down along the way, always returning to Thomas's economic conceptions, every aspect of which he tries to bring out. This is the case, for example, when he invites us to read the *Commentary on the Book of Isaiah*, which Thomas Aquinas wrote in his youth in order to clarify the risk on exchange ratio, or when he relies on Thomas's theology of sacraments in order to refine his conception of the just price.

In this book, Pierre Januard therefore overcomes the two above-mentioned obstacles, relating respectively to the level of investigation and to the boundaries of economics. And that is undoubtedly the best way to serve the author he is dealing with: he invites us to read Thomas Aquinas, seeking the same kind of analytical elements that we would have sought in other economists of the past who have left their mark on our discipline.

André Lapidus,
Professor Emeritus of Economics,
University Paris 1 Panthéon-Sorbonne

References

Fiévet, Amélie. 2022. Decision over Time as a By-Product of a Measure of Utility: A Reappraisal of Paul Samuelson's 'A Note on Measurement of Utility' (1937). European Journal of the History of Economic Thought 29 (3): 438–454.

Fishburn, Peter C., and Rubinstein, Ariel. 1982. Time Preference. *International Economic Review* 23 (3): 677–694.

Samuelson, Paul A. 1937. A Note on Measurement of Utility. *Review of Economic Studies* 4 (2): 155–161.

Skinner, Quentin. 1969. Meaning and Understanding in the History of Ideas. *History and Theory* 8: 3–53.

The manufacturer's authorised representative in the EU is Springer
Nature Customer Service Centre GmbH, Europaplatz 3, 69115 Heidelberg,
Germany. If you have any concerns regarding our products, please
contact ProductSafety@springernature.com

Printed and bound by CPI Group (UK) Ltd, Croydon, CR0 4YY
01/10/2026
02225978-0010